The History of Josephine

The History of Josephine

Makers of History Series

Jacob Abbott

Cedar Lake Classics

CONTENTS

PREFACE vii
PHOTO INSERT viii

1. Life in Martinique 1
2. Marriage of Josephine 11
3. Arrest of M. Beauharnais and Josephine 21
4. Scenes in Prison 32
5. The Release from Prison 39
6. Josephine in Italy 52
7. Josephine at Malmaison 65
8. Josephine the Wife of the First Consul 76
9. Developments of Character 88
10. The Coronation 104
11. Josephine and Empress 123
12. The Divorce and Last Days 151

CONTENTS

ABOUT JACOB ABBOTT **179**
BIOGRAPHIES ABBOTT WROTE **181**

PREFACE

Marie Antoinette, Madame Roland, and Josephine are the three most prominent heroines of the French Revolution. The history of their lives necessarily records all the most interesting events of that most fearful tragedy which man has ever enacted. Marie Antoinette beheld the morning dawn of the Revolution; its lurid mid-day sun glared upon Madame Roland; and Josephine beheld the portentous phenomenon fade away. Each of these heroines displayed traits of character worthy of all imitation. No one can read the history of their lives without being ennobled by the contemplation of the fortitude and grandeur of spirit they evinced. To the young ladies of our land we especially commend these Heroines of the French Revolution.

JOSEPHINE.

1

Life in Martinique

he island of Martinique emerges in tropical luxuriance from the bosom of the Caribbean Sea. A meridian sun causes the whole land to smile in perennial verdure, and all the gorgeous flowers and luscious fruits of the torrid zone adorn upland and prairie in boundless profusion. Mountains, densely wooded, rear their summits sublimely to the skies, and valleys charm the eye with pictures more beautiful than imagination can create. Ocean breezes ever sweep these hills and vales, and temper the heat of a vertical sun. Slaves, whose dusky limbs are scarcely veiled by the lightest clothing, till the soil, while the white inhabitants, supported by the indolent labor of these unpaid menials, loiter away life in listless leisure and in rustic luxury. Far removed from the dissipating influences of European and American opulence, they dwell in their secluded island in a state of almost patriarchal simplicity.

About the year 1760, a young French officer, Captain Joseph Gaspard Tascher, accompanied his regiment of horse to this island. While here on professional duty, he became attached to a young lady from France, whose parents, formerly opulent, in consequence of the loss of property, had moved to the West Indies to retrieve their fortunes. But little is known respecting Mademoiselle de Sanois, this young lady, who was soon married to M. Tascher. Josephine was the only child born of this union. In consequence of the early death of her mother, she was, while an infant, intrusted to the care of her aunt. Her father soon after died, and the little orphan appears never to have known a father's or a mother's love.

Madame Renaudin, the kind aunt, who now, with maternal affection, took charge of the helpless infant, was a lady of wealth, and of great benevolence of character. Her husband was the owner of several estates, and lived surrounded by all that plain and rustic profusion which characterizes the abode of the wealthy planter. His large possessions, and his energy of character, gave him a wide influence over the island. He was remarkable for his humane treatment of his slaves, and for the successful manner with which he conducted the affairs of his plantations.

The general condition of the slaves of Martinique at this time was very deplorable; but on the plantations of M. Renaudin there was as perfect a state of contentment and of happiness as is consistent with the deplorable institution of slavery. The slaves, many of them but recently torn from their homes in Africa, were necessarily ignorant, degraded, and superstitious. They knew nothing of those more elevated and refined enjoyments which the cultivated mind so highly appreciates, but which are so often also connected with the most exquisite suffering. Josephine, in subsequent life, gave a very vivid description of the wretchedness of the slaves in general, and also of the peace and harmony which, in striking contrast, cheered the estates of her uncle. When the days' tasks were done, the negroes, constitutionally light-hearted and merry, gathered around their cabins with songs and dances, often prolonged late into the hours of the night. They had never known any thing better than their present lot. They compared their condition with that of the slaves on the adjoining plantations, and exulted in view of their own enjoyments. M. and Madame Renaudin often visited their cabins, spoke words of kindness to them in their hours of sickness and sorrow, encouraged the formation of pure attachments and honorable marriage among the young, and took a lively interest in their sports. The slaves loved their kind master and mistress most sincerely, and manifested their affection in a thousand simple ways which touched the heart.

Josephine imbibed from infancy the spirit of her uncle and aunt. She always spoke to the slaves in tones of kindness, and became a universal favorite with all upon the plantations. She had no playmates but the little negroes and she united with them freely in all their sports. Still, these little ebon children of bondage evidently looked up to Josephine as to a superior being. She was the queen around whom they circled in affectionate homage. The instinctive faculty, which Josephine displayed through life, of winning the most ardent love of all who met her, while, at the same time, she was protected from any undue familiarity, she seems to have possessed even at that early day. The children, who were her companions in all the sports of childhood, were also dutiful subjects ever ready to be obedient to her will.

The social position of M. Renaudin, as one of the most opulent and influential gentlemen of Martinique, necessarily attracted to his hospitable residence much refined and cultivated society. Strangers from Europe visiting the island, planters of intellectual tastes, and ladies of polished manners, met a cordial welcome beneath the spacious roof of this abode, where all abundance was to be found. Madame Renaudin had passed her early years in Paris, and her manners were embellished with that elegance and refinement which have given to Parisian society such a world-wide celebrity. There was, at that period, much more intercourse between the mother country and the colonies than at the present day. Thus Josephine, though reared in a provincial home, was accustomed, from infancy, to associate with gentlemen and ladies who were familiar with the etiquette of the highest rank in society, and whose conversation was intellectual and improving.

It at first view seems difficult to account for the high degree of mental culture which Josephine displayed, when, seated by the side of Napoleon, she was the Empress of France. Her remarks, her letters, her conversational elegance, gave indication of a mind thoroughly furnished with information and trained by severe discipline. And yet, from all the glimpses we can catch of her early education, it would seem that, with the exception of the accomplishments of music, dancing, and drawing, she was left very much to the guidance of her own instinctive tastes. But, like Madame Roland, she was blessed with that peculiar mental constitution, which led her, of her own accord, to treasure up all knowledge which books or conversation brought within her reach. From childhood until the hour of her death, she was ever improving her mind by careful observation and studious reading. She played upon the harp with great skill, and sang with a voice of exquisite melody. She also read with a correctness of elocution and a fervor of feeling which ever attracted admiration. The morning of her childhood was indeed bright and sunny, and her gladdened heart became so habituated to joyousness, that her cheerful spirit seldom failed her even in the darkest days of her calamity. Her passionate love for flowers had interested her deeply in the study of botany, and she also became very skillful in embroidery, that accomplishment which was once deemed an essential part of the education of every lady.

Under such influences Josephine became a child of such grace, beauty, and loveliness of character as to attract the attention and the admiration of all who saw her. There was an affectionateness, simplicity, and frankness in her manners which won all hearts. Her most intimate companion in these early years was a young mulatto girl, the daughter of a slave, and report said, with how much truth it is impossible to know, that she was also the daughter of Captain Tascher before his marriage. Her name was Euphemie. She was a year or two older than Josephine, but she attached herself with deathless affection to her patroness; and, though Josephine made her a companion and a confidante, she gradually passed, even in these early years, into the position of a maid of honor, and clung devotedly to her mistress through all the changes of subsequent life. Josephine, at this time secluded from all companionship with young ladies of her own rank and age, made this humble but active-minded and intelligent girl her bosom companion. They rambled together, the youthful mistress and her maid, in perfect harmony. From Josephine's more highly-cultivated mind the lowly-born child derived intellectual stimulus, and thus each day became a more worthy and congenial associate. As years passed on, and Josephine ascended into higher regions of splendor, her humble attendant gradually retired into more obscure positions, though she was ever regarded by her true-hearted mistress with great kindness.

Josephine was a universal favorite with all the little negro girls of the plantation. They looked up to her as to a protectress whom they loved, and to whom they owed entire homage. She would frequently collect a group of them under the shade of the luxuriant trees of that tropical island, and teach them the dances which she had learned, and also join with them as a partner. She loved to assemble them around her, and listen to those simple negro melodies which penetrate every heart which can feel the power of music. Again, all their voices, in sweet harmony, blended with hers as she taught them the more scientific songs of Europe. She would listen with unaffected interest to their tales of sorrow, and weep with them. Often she interposed in their behalf that their tasks might be lightened, or that a play-day might be allowed them. Thus she was as much beloved and admired in the cabin of the poor negro as she was in her uncle's parlor, where intelligence and refinement were assembled. This same character she displayed through the whole of her career. Josephine upon the plantation and Josephine upon the throne—Josephine surrounded by the sable maidens of Martinique, and Josephine moving in queenly splendor in the palaces of Versailles, with all the courtiers of Europe revolving around her, displayed the same traits of character, and by her unaffected kindness won the hearts alike of the lowly and of the exalted.

About this time an occurrence took place which has attracted far more attention than it deserves. Josephine was one day walking under the shade of the trees of the plantation, when she saw a number of negro children gathered around an aged and withered negress, who had great reputation among the slaves as a fortune-teller. Curiosity induced Josephine to draw near the group to hear what the sorceress had to say. The old sibyl, with the cunning which is characteristic of her craft, as soon as she saw Josephine approach, whom she knew perfectly, assumed an air of great agitation, and, seizing her hand violently, gazed with most earnest attention upon the lines traced upon the palm. The little negresses were perfectly awe-stricken by this oracular display. Josephine, however, was only amused, and smiling, said,

"So you discover something very extraordinary in my destiny?"

"Yes!" replied the negress, with an air of great solemnity.

"Is happiness or misfortune to be my lot?" Josephine inquired.

The negress again gazed upon her hand, and then replied, "Misfortune;" but, after a moment's pause, she added, "and happiness too."

"You must be careful, my good woman," Josephine rejoined, "not to commit yourself. Your predictions are not very intelligible."

The negress, raising her eyes with an expression of deep mystery to heaven, rejoined, "I am not permitted to render my revelations more clear."

In every human heart there is a vein of credulity. The pretended prophetess had now succeeded in fairly arousing the curiosity of Josephine, who eagerly inquired, "What do you read respecting me in futurity? Tell me exactly."

The Sibyl.

Again the negress, assuming an air of profound solemnity, said, "You will not believe me if I reveal to you your strange destiny."

"Yes, indeed, I assure you that I will," Josephine thoughtlessly replied. "Come, good mother, do tell me what I have to hope and what to fear."

"On your own head be it, then. Listen. You will soon be married. That union will not be happy. You will become a widow, and then you will be Queen of France. Some happy years will be yours, but afterward you will die in a hospital, amid civil commotions."

The old woman then hurried away. Josephine talked a few moments with the young negroes upon the folly of this pretended fortune-telling, and leaving them, the affair passed from her mind. In subsequent years, when toiling through the vicissitudes of her most eventful life, she recalled the singular coincidence between her destiny and the prediction, and seemed to consider that the negress, with prophetic vision, had traced out her wonderful career.

But what is there so extraordinary in this narrative? What maiden ever consulted a fortune-teller without receiving the agreeable announcement that she was to wed beauty, and wealth, and rank? It was known universally, and it was a constant subject of plantation gossip, that the guardians of Josephine were contemplating a match for her with the son of a neighboring planter. The negroes did not think him half worthy of their adored and queenly Josephine. They supposed, however, that the match was settled. The artful woman was therefore compelled to allow Josephine to marry *at first* the undistinguished son of the planter, with whom she could not be happy. She, however, very considerately lets the unworthy husband in a short time die, and then Josephine becomes a queen. This is the old story, which has been repeated to half the maidens in Christendom. It is not very surprising that in this one case it should have happened to prove true.

But, unfortunately, our prophetess went a little farther, and predicted that Josephine would die in a hospital—implying poverty and abandonment. This part of the prediction proved to be utterly untrue. Josephine, instead of dying in a hospital, died in the beautiful palace of Malmaison. Instead of dying in poverty, she was one of the richest ladies in Europe, receiving an income of some six hundred thousand dollars a year. The grounds around her palace were embellished with all the attractions, and her apartments furnished with every luxury which opulence could provide. Instead of dying in friendlessness and neglect, the Emperor Alexander of Russia stood at her bed-side; the most illustrious kings and nobles of Europe crowded her court and did her homage. And though she was separated from her husband, she still retained the title of Empress, and was the object of his most sincere affection and esteem.

Thus this prediction, upon which so much stress has been laid, seems to vanish in the air. It surely is not a supernatural event that a young lady, who was told by an aged negress that she would be a queen, happened actually to become one.

We have alluded to a contemplated match between Josephine and the son of a neighboring planter. An English family, who had lost property and rank in the convulsions of those times, had sought a retreat in the island of Martinique, and were cultivating an adjoining plantation. In this family there was a very pleasant lad, a son, of nearly the same age with Josephine. The plantations being near to each other, they were often companions and playmates. A strong attachment grew up between them. The parents of William, and the uncle and aunt of Josephine, approved cordially of this attachment; and were desirous that these youthful hearts should be united, as soon as the parties should arrive at mature age. Josephine, in the ingenuous artlessness of her nature, disguised not in the least her strong affection for William. And his attachment to her was deep and enduring. The solitude of their lives peculiarly tended to promote fervor of character.

Matters were in this state, when the father of William received an intimation from England that, by returning to his own country, he might, perhaps, regain his lost estates. He immediately prepared to leave the island with his family. The separation was a severe blow to these youthful lovers. They wept, and vowed eternal fidelity.

THE HISTORY OF JOSEPHINE

It is not surprising that Josephine should have been in some degree superstitious. The peculiarity of her life upon the plantation—her constant converse with the negroes, whose minds were imbued with all the superstitious notions which they had brought from Africa, united with those which they had found upon the island, tended to foster those feelings. Rousseau, the most popular and universally-read French writer of that day, in his celebrated "Confessions," records with perfect composure that he was one day sitting in a grove, meditating whether his soul would probably be saved or lost. He felt that the question was of the utmost importance. How could he escape from the uncertainty! A supernatural voice seemed to suggest an appeal to a singular kind of augury. "I will," said he, "throw this stone at that tree. If I hit the tree, it shall be a sign that my soul is to be saved. If I miss it, it shall indicate that I am to be lost." He selected a large tree, took the precaution of getting very near to it, and threw his stone plump against the trunk. "After that," says the philosopher, "I never again had a doubt respecting my salvation."

Josephine resorted to the same kind of augury to ascertain if William, who had become a student in the University at Oxford, still remained faithful to her. She not unfrequently attempted to beguile a weary hour in throwing pebbles at the trees, that she might divine whether William were then thinking of her. Months, however, passed away, and she received no tidings from him. Though she had often written, her letters remained unanswered. Her feelings were the more deeply wounded, since there were other friends upon the island with whom he kept up a correspondence; but Josephine never received even a message through them.

One day, as she was pensively rambling in a grove, where she had often walked with her absent lover, she found carved upon a tree the names of William and Josephine. She knew well by whose hand they had been cut, and, entirely overcome with emotion, she sat down and wept bitterly. With the point of a knife, and with a trembling hand, she inscribed in the bark these words, peculiarly characteristic of her depth of feeling, and of the gentleness of her spirit: "Unhappy William! thou hast forgotten me!"

William, however, had not forgotten her. Again and again he had written in terms of the most ardent affection. But the friends of Josephine, meeting with an opportunity for a match for her which they deemed far more advantageous, had destroyed these communications, and also had prevented any of her letters from reaching the hand of William. Thus each, while cherishing the truest affection, deemed the other faithless.

2

Marriage of Josephine

Josephine was about fourteen years of age when she was separated from William. A year passed away, during which she received not a line from her absent friend. About this time a gentleman from France visited her uncle upon business of great importance. Viscount Alexander de Beauharnais was a fashionable and gallant young man, about thirty years of age, possessing much conversational ease and grace of manner, and accustomed to the most polished society of the French metropolis. He held a commission in the army, and had already signalized himself by several acts of bravery. His sympathies had been strongly aroused by the struggle of the American colonists with the mother country, and he had already aided the colonists both with his sword and his purse.

Several large and valuable estates in Martinique, adjoining the plantation of M. Renaudin, had fallen by inheritance to this young officer and his brother, the Marquis of Beauharnais. He visited Martinique to secure the proof of his title to these estates. M. Renaudin held some of these plantations on lease. In the transaction of this business, Beauharnais spent much time at the mansion of M. Renaudin. He, of course, saw much of the beautiful Josephine, and was fascinated with her grace, and her mental and physical loveliness.

The uncle and aunt of Josephine were delighted to perceive the interest which their niece had awakened in the bosom of the interesting stranger. His graceful figure, his accomplished person, his military celebrity, his social rank, and his large fortune, all conspired to dazzle their eyes, and to lead them to do every thing in their power to promote a match apparently so eligible. The ambition of M. Renaudin was moved at the thought of conferring upon his niece, the prospective heiress of his own fortune, an estate so magnificent as the united inheritance. Josephine, however, had not yet forgotten William, and, though interested in her uncle's guest, for some time allowed no emotion of love to flow out toward him.

One morning Josephine was sitting in the library in pensive musings, when her uncle came into the room to open to her the subject of her contemplated marriage with M. Beauharnais. Josephine was thunderstruck at the communication, for, according to the invariable custom of the times, she knew that she could have but little voice in the choice of a partner for life. For a short time she listened in silence to his proposals, and then said, with tears in her eyes,

"Dear uncle, I implore you to remember that my affections are fixed upon William. I have been solemnly promised to him."

"That is utterly impossible, my child," her uncle replied. "Circumstances are changed. All our hopes are centered in you. You must obey our wishes."

"And why," said she, "have you changed your intentions in reference to William?"

Her uncle replied: "You will receive by inheritance all my estate. M. Beauharnais possesses the rich estates adjoining. Your union unites the property. M. Beauharnais is every thing which can be desired in a husband. Besides, William appears to have forgotten you."

To this last remark Josephine could make no reply. She looked sadly upon the floor and was silent. It is said that her uncle had then in his possession several letters which William had written her, replete with the most earnest spirit of constancy and affection.

Josephine, but fifteen years of age, could not, under these circumstances, resist the influences now brought to bear upon her. M. Beauharnais was a gentleman of fascinating accomplishments. The reluctance of Josephine to become his bride but stimulated his zeal to obtain her. In the seclusion of the plantation, and far removed from other society, she was necessarily with him nearly at all hours. They read together, rode on horseback side by side, rambled in the groves in pleasant companionship. They floated by moonlight upon the water, breathing the balmy air of that delicious clime, and uniting their voices in song, the measure being timed with the dipping of the oars by the negroes. The friends of Josephine were importunate for the match. At last, reluctantly she gave her consent. Having done this, she allowed her affections, unrestrained, to repose upon her betrothed. Though her heart still clung to William, she thought that he had found other friends in England, in whose pleasant companionship he had lost all remembrance of the island maiden who had won his early love.

Alexander Beauharnais, soon after his engagement to Josephine, embarked for France. Arrangements had been made for Josephine, in the course of a few months, to follow him, upon a visit to a relative in Paris, and there the nuptials were to be consummated. Josephine was now fifteen years of age. She was attached to Beauharnais, but not with that fervor of feeling which had previously agitated her heart. She often thought of William and spoke of him, and at times had misgivings lest there might be some explanation of his silence. But months had passed on, and she had received no letter or message from him.

At length the hour for her departure from the island arrived. With tearful eyes and a saddened heart she left the land of her birth, and the scenes endeared to her by all the recollections of childhood. Groups of negroes, from the tottering infant to the aged man of gray hairs, surrounded her with weeping and loud lamentation. Josephine hastened on board, the ship got under way, and soon the island of Martinique disappeared beneath the watery horizon. Josephine sat upon the deck in perfect silence, watching the dim outline of her beloved home till it was lost to sight. Her young heart was full of anxiety, of tenderness, and of regrets. Little, however, could she imagine the career of strange vicissitudes upon which she was about to enter.

The voyage was long and tempestuous. Storms pursued them all the way. At one time the ship was dismasted and came near foundering. At length the welcome cry of "Land" was heard, and Josephine, an unknown orphan child of fifteen, placed her feet upon the shores of France, that country over which she was soon to reign the most renowned empress. She hastened to Fontainebleau, and was there met by Alexander Beauharnais. He received her with great fondness, and was assiduous in bestowing upon her the most flattering attentions. But Josephine had hardly arrived at Fontainebleau before she heard that William and his father were also residing at that place. Her whole frame trembled like an aspen leaf, and her heart sunk within her as she received the intelligence. All her long-cherished affection for the companion of her childhood was revived, and still she knew not but that William was faithless. He, however, immediately called, with his father, to see her. The interview was most embarrassing, for each loved the other intensely, and each had reason to believe that the other had proved untrue. The next day William called alone; Josephine, the betrothed bride of Beauharnais, prudently declined seeing him. He then wrote her a letter, which he bribed a servant to place in her hands, full of protestations of love, stating how he had written to her, and passionately inquiring why she turned so coldly from him.

Josephine read the letter with a bursting heart. She now saw how she had been deceived. She now was convinced that William had proved faithful to her, notwithstanding he had so much reason to believe that she had been untrue to him. But what could she do? She was but fifteen years of age. She was surrounded only by those who were determined that she should marry Alexander Beauharnais. She was told that the friends of William had decided unalterably that he should marry an English heiress, and that the fortunes of his father's family were dependent upon that alliance. The servant who had been the bearer of William's epistle was dismissed, and the other servants were commanded not to allow him to enter the house.

The agitation of Josephine's heart was such that for some time she was unable to leave her bed. She entreated her friends to allow her for a few months to retire to a convent, that she might, in solitary thought and prayer, regain composure. Her friends consented to this arrangement, and she took refuge in the convent at Panthemont. Here she spent a few months in inexpressible gloom. William made many unavailing efforts to obtain an interview, and at last, in despair, reluctantly received the wealthy bride, through whom he secured an immense inheritance, and with whom he passed an unloving life.

The Viscount Beauharnais often called to see her, and was permitted to converse with her at the gate of her window. In the simplicity of her heart, she told her friends at the convent of her attachment for William; how they had been reared together, and how they had loved from childhood. She felt that it was a cruel fate which separated them, but a fate before which each must inevitably bow. At last she calmly made up her mind to comply with the wishes of her friends, and to surrender herself to the Viscount Beauharnais. There was much in the person and character of Beauharnais to render him very attractive, and she soon became sincerely, though never passionately, attached to him.

Josephine was sixteen years of age when she was married. Her social position was in the midst of the most expensive and fashionable society of Paris. She was immediately involved in all the excitements of parties, and balls, and gorgeous entertainments. Her beauty, her grace, her amiability, and her peculiarly musical voice, which fell like a charm upon every ear, excited great admiration and not a little envy. It was a dangerous scene into which to introduce the artless and inexperienced Creole girl, and she was not a little dazzled by the splendor with which she was surrounded. Every thing that could minister to convenience, or that could gratify taste, was lavished profusely around her. For a time she was bewildered by the novelty of her situation. But soon she became weary of the heartless pageantry of fashionable life, and sighed for the tranquil enjoyments of her island home.

Her husband, proud of her beauty and accomplishments, introduced her at court. Maria Antoinette, who had then just ascended the throne, and was in the brilliance of her youth, and beauty, and early popularity, was charmed with the West Indian bride, and received her without the formality of a public presentation. When these two young brides met in the regal palace of Versailles—the one a daughter of Maria Theresa and a descendant of the Cæsars, who had come from the court of Austria to be not only the queen, but the brightest ornament of the court of France—the other the child of a planter, born upon an obscure island, reared in the midst of negresses, as almost her only companions —little did they imagine that Maria Antoinette was to go down, down, down to the lowest state of ignominy and woe, while Josephine was to ascend to more and more exalted stations, until she should sit upon a throne more glorious than the Cæsars ever knew.

French philosophy had at this time undermined the religion of Jesus Christ. All that is sacred in the domestic relations was withering beneath the blight of infidelity. Beauharnais, a man of fashion and of the world, had imbibed, to the full, the sentiments which disgraced the age. Marriage was deemed a partnership, to be formed or dissolved at pleasure. Fidelity to the nuptial tie was the jest of philosophers and witlings. Josephine had soon the mortification of seeing a proud, beautiful, and artful woman taking her place, and openly and triumphantly claiming the attentions and the affections of her husband. This woman, high in rank, loved to torture her poor victim. "Your dear Alexander," she said to Josephine, "daily lavishes upon others the tribute of attachment which you think he reserves solely for you." She could not bear to see the beautiful and virtuous Josephine happy, as the honored wife of her guilty lover, and she resolved, if possible, to sow the seeds of jealousy so effectually between them as to secure a separation.

In the year 1780 Josephine gave birth to her daughter Hortense. This event seemed for a time to draw back the wandering affections of Beauharnais. He was really proud of his wife. He admired her beauty and her grace. He doted upon his infant daughter. But he was an infidel.

He recognized no law of God, commanding purity of heart and life, and he contended that Josephine had no right to complain, as long as he treated her kindly, if he did indulge in the waywardness of passion.

The path of Josephine was now, indeed, shrouded in gloom, and each day seemed to grow darker and darker. Hortense became her idol and her only comfort. Her husband lavished upon her those luxuries which his wealth enabled him to grant. He was kind to her in words and in all the ordinary courtesies of intercourse. But Josephine's heart was well-nigh broken. A few years of conflict passed slowly away, when she gave birth, in the year 1783, to her son Eugene. In the society of her children the unhappy mother found now her only solace.

While the Viscount Beauharnais was ready to defend his own conduct, he was by no means willing that his wife should govern herself by the same principles of fashionable philosophy. The code infidel is got up for the especial benefit of dissolute *men*; their *wives* must be governed by another code. The artful woman, who was the prime agent in these difficulties, affected great sympathy with Josephine in her sorrows, protested her own entire innocence, but assured her that M. Beauharnais was an ingrate, entirely unworthy of her affections. She deceived Josephine, hoarded up the confidence of her stricken heart, and conversed with her about *William*, the memory of whose faithful love now came with new freshness to the disconsolate wife.

Josephine, lured by her, wrote a letter to her friends in Martinique, in which she imprudently said, "Were it not for my children, I should without a pang, renounce France forever. My duty requires me to forget William; and yet if *we* had been united together, I should not to-day have been troubling you with my griefs."

The woman who instigated her to write this letter was infamous enough to obtain it by stealth and show it to Beauharnais. His jealousy and indignation were immediately aroused to the highest pitch. He was led by this malicious deceiver to believe that Josephine had obtained secret interviews with William, and the notoriously unfaithful husband was exasperated to the highest degree at the very suspicion of the want of fidelity in his wife. He reproached her in language of the utmost severity, took Eugene from her, and resolved to endeavor, by legal process, to obtain an entire divorce. She implored him, for the sake of her children, not to proclaim their difficulties to the world. He, however, reckless of consequences, made application to the courts for the annulment of the matrimonial bond. Josephine was now compelled to defend her own character. She again retired with Hortense to the convent, and there, through dreary months of solitude, and silence, and dejection, awaited the result of the trial upon which her reputation as a virtuous woman was staked. The decree of the court was triumphantly in her favor, and Josephine returned to her friends to receive their congratulations, but impressed with the conviction that earth had no longer a joy in store for her. Her friends did all in their power to cheer her desponding spirit; but the wound she had received was too deep to be speedily healed. One day her friends, to divert her mind from brooding over irreparable sorrows, took her, almost by violence, to Versailles. They passed over the enchanting grounds, and through the gorgeously-furnished apartments of the Great and Little Trianon, the favorite haunts of Maria Antoinette. Here the beautiful Queen of France was accustomed to lay aside the pageantry of royalty, and to enjoy, without restraint, the society of those who were dear to her. Days of darkness and trouble had already begun to darken around her path. As Josephine was looking at some of the works of art, she was greatly surprised at the entrance of the queen, surrounded by several ladies of her court. Maria Antoinette immediately recognized Josephine, and with that air of affability and kindness which ever characterized her conduct, she approached her, and, with one of her winning smiles, said, "Madame Beauharnais, I am very happy to see you at the two Trianons. You well know how to appreciate their beauties. I should be much pleased to learn what objects you consider most interesting. I shall always receive you with pleasure."

These words from the queen were an unspeakable solace to Josephine. Her afflicted heart needed the consolation. The queen was acquainted with her trials, and thus nobly assured her of her sympathy and her confidence. In a few days Maria Antoinette invited Josephine to a private interview. She addressed her in words of the utmost kindness, promised to watch over the interests of her son, and at the same time, as a mark of her especial regard, she took from her neck an antique ornament of precious stones, and passed it over the neck of Josephine. The king also himself came in at the interview, for his heart had been softened by sorrow, and addressed words of consolation to the injured and discarded wife.

Josephine now received letters from Martinique earnestly entreating her to return, with her children, to the home of her childhood. World-weary, she immediately resolved to accept the invitation. But the thought of crossing the wide ocean, and leaving her son Eugene behind, was a severe pang to a mother's heart. Eugene had been taken from her and sent to a boarding-school. Josephine felt so deeply the pang of separation from her beloved child, that she obtained an interview with M. Beauharnais, and implored him to allow her to take Eugene with her. He gave a cold and positive refusal.

A few days after this, Josephine, cruelly separated from her husband and bereaved of her son, embarked with Hortense for Martinique. She strove to maintain that aspect of cheerfulness and of dignity which an injured but innocent woman is entitled to exhibit. When dark hours of despondency overshadowed her, she tried to console herself with the beautiful thought of Plautus: "If we support adversity with courage, we shall have a keener relish for returning prosperity." It does not appear that she had any refuge in the consolations of religion. She had a vague and general idea of the goodness of a superintending Providence, but she was apparently a stranger to those warm and glowing revelations of Christianity which introduce us to a sympathizing Savior, a guiding and consoling Spirit, a loving and forgiving Father. Could she then, by faith, have reposed her aching head upon the bosom of her heavenly Father, she might have found a solace such as nothing else could confer. But at this time nearly every mind in France was more or less darkened by the glooms of infidelity.

The winds soon drove her frail bark across the Atlantic, and Josephine, pale and sorrow-stricken, was clasped in the arms and folded to the hearts of those who truly loved her. The affectionate negroes gathered around her, with loud demonstrations of their sympathy and their joy in again meeting their mistress. Here, amid the quiet scenes endeared to her by the recollections of childhood, she found a temporary respite from those storms by which she had been so severely tossed upon life's wild and tempestuous ocean.

3

Arrest of M. Beauharnais and Josephine

Josephine remained in Martinique three years. She passed her time in tranquil sadness, engaged in reading, in educating Hortense, and in unwearied acts of kindness to those around her. Like all noble minds, she had a great fondness for the beauties of nature. The luxuriant groves of the tropics, the serene skies which overarched her head, the gentle zephyrs which breathed through orange groves, all were congenial with her pensive spirit. The thought of Eugene, her beautiful boy, so far from her, preyed deeply upon her heart. Often she retired alone to some of those lonely walks which she loved so well, and wept over her alienated husband and her lost child.

M. Beauharnais surrendered himself for a time, without restraint, to every indulgence. He tried, in the society of sin and shame, to forget his wife and his absent daughter. He, however, soon found that no friend can take the place of a virtuous and an affectionate wife. The memory of Josephine's gentleness, and tenderness, and love came flooding back upon his heart. He became fully convinced of his injustice to her, and earnestly desired to have her restored again to him and to his home. He sent communications to Josephine, expressive of his deep regret for the past, promising amendment for the future, assuring her of his high appreciation of her elevated and honorable character, and imploring her to return with Hortense, thus to reunite the divided and sorrow-stricken household. It was indeed a gratification to Josephine to receive from her husband the acknowledgment that she had never ceased to deserve his confidence. The thought of again pressing Eugene to her bosom filled a mother's heart with rapture. Still, the griefs which had weighed upon her were so heavy, that she confessed to her friends that, were it not for the love which she bore Eugene, she would greatly prefer to spend the remnant of her days upon her favorite island. Her friends did every thing in their power to dissuade her from leaving Martinique. But a mother's undying love triumphed, and again she embarked for France.

In subsequent years, when surrounded by all the splendors of royalty, she related to some of the ladies of her court, with that unaffected simplicity which ever marked her character, the following incident, which occurred during this voyage. The ladies were admiring some brilliant jewels which were spread out before them. Josephine said to them, "My young friends, believe me, splendor does not constitute happiness. I at one time received greater enjoyment from the gift of a pair of old shoes than all these diamonds have ever afforded me." The curiosity of her auditors was, of course, greatly excited, and they entreated her to explain her meaning.

"Yes, young ladies," Josephine continued, "of all the presents I ever received, the one which gave me the greatest pleasure was *a pair of old shoes, and those, too, of coarse leather*. When I last returned to France from Martinique, having separated from my first husband, I was far from rich. The passage-money exhausted my resources, and it was not without difficulty that I obtained the indispensable requisites for our voyage. Hortense, obliging and lively, performing with much agility the dances of the negroes, and singing their songs with surprising correctness, greatly amused the sailors, who, from being her constant play-fellows, had become her favorite society. An old sailor became particularly attached to the child, and she doted upon the old man. What with running, leaping, and walking, my daughter's slight shoes were fairly worn out. Knowing that she had not another pair, and fearing I would forbid her going upon deck, should this defect in her attire be discovered, Hortense carefully concealed the disaster. One day I experienced the distress of seeing her return from the deck leaving every foot-mark in blood. When examining how matters stood, I found her shoes literally in tatters, and her feet dreadfully torn by a nail. We were as yet not more than half way across the ocean, and it seemed impossible to procure another pair of shoes. I felt quite overcome at the idea of the sorrow my poor Hortense would suffer, as also at the danger to which her health might be exposed by confinement in my miserable little cabin. At this moment our good friend, the old sailor, entered and inquired the cause of our distress. Hortense, sobbing all the while, eagerly informed him that she could no more go upon deck, for her shoes were worn out, and mamma had no others to give her. 'Nonsense,' said the worthy seaman, 'is that all? I have an old pair somewhere in my chest; I will go and seek them. You, madam, can cut them to shape, and I will splice them up as well as need be.' Without waiting for a reply, away hastened the kind sailor in search of his old shoes; these he soon after brought to us with a triumphant air, and they were received by Hortense with demonstrations of the most lively joy. We set to work with all zeal, and before the day closed my daughter could resume her delightful duties of supplying their evening's diversion to the crew. I again repeat, never was present received with greater thankfulness. It has since often been matter of self-reproach that I did not particularly inquire into the name and history of our benefactor. It would have been gratifying for me to have done something for him when afterward means were in my power."

Poor Hortense! most wonderful were the vicissitudes of her checkered and joyless life. We here meet her, almost an infant, in poverty and obscurity. The mother and child arrive in Paris on the morning of that Reign of Terror, the story of which has made the ear of humanity to tingle. Hortense is deprived of both her parents, and is left in friendlessness and beggary in the streets of Paris. A charitable neighbor cherished and fed her. Her mother is liberated, and married to Napoleon; and

Hortense, as daughter of the emperor, is surrounded with dazzling splendor, such as earth has seldom witnessed. We now meet Hortense, radiant in youthful beauty, one of the most admired and courted in the midst of the glittering throng, which, like a fairy vision, dazzles all eyes in the gorgeous apartments of Versailles and St. Cloud. Her person is adorned with the most costly fabrics and the most brilliant gems which Europe can afford. The nobles and princes of the proudest courts vie with each other for the honor of her hand. She is led to her sumptuous bridals by Louis Bonaparte, brother of the emperor; becomes the spouse of a king, and takes her seat upon the throne of Holland. But in the midst of all this external splendor she is wretched at heart. Not one congenial feeling unites her with the companion to whom she is bound. Louis, weary of regal pomp and constraint, abdicates the throne, and Hortense becomes unendurably weary of her pensive and unambitious spouse. They agree to separate; each to journey along, unattended by the other, the remainder of life's pilgrimage. Hortense seeks a joyless refuge in a secluded castle, in one of the most retired valleys of Switzerland. The tornado of counter-revolution sweeps over Europe, and all her exalted friends and towering hopes are prostrated in the dust. Lingering years of disappointment and sadness pass over her, and old age, with its infirmities, places her upon a dying bed. One only child, Louis Napoleon, since President of the French Republic, the victim of corroding ambition and ceaselessly-gnawing discontent, stands at her bed-side to close her eyes, and to follow her, a solitary and lonely mourner, to the grave. The dream of life has passed. The shadow has vanished away. Who can fathom the mystery of the creation of such a drama?

Josephine arrived in France. She was received most cordially by her husband. Sorrowful experience had taught him the value of a home, and the worth of a pure and a sanctified love. Josephine again folded her idolized Eugene in her arms, and the anguish of past years was forgotten in the blissful enjoyments of a reunited family. These bright and happy days were, however, soon again clouded. The French Revolution was now in full career. The king and queen were in prison. All law was prostrate. M. Beauharnais, at the commencement of the Revolution, had most cordially espoused the cause of popular liberty. He stood by the side of La Fayette a companion and a supporter. His commanding character gave him great influence. He was elected a deputy to the Constituent Assembly, and took an active part in its proceedings. Upon the dissolution of this Assembly, or States-General, as it was also called, as by vote none of its members were immediately re-eligible, he retired again to the army; but when the second or Legislative Assembly was dissolved and the National Convention was formed, he was returned as a member, and at two successive sessions was elected its president.

The people, having obtained an entire victory over monarchy and aristocracy, beheaded the king and queen, and drove the nobles from the realm. France was now divided into two great parties. The Jacobins were so called from an old cloister in which they at first held their meetings. All of the lowest, most vicious, and the reckless of the nation belonged to this party. They seemed disposed to overthrow all law, human and divine. Marat, Danton, and Robespierre were the blood-stained leaders of this wild and furious faction. The Girondists, their opponents, were so called from the department of the Gironde, from which most of the leaders of this party came. They wished for a republic like that of the United States, where there should be the protection of life, and property, and liberty, with healthy laws sacredly enforced.

The conflict between the two parties was long and terrible. The Jacobins gained the victory, and the Girondists were led to the guillotine. M. Beauharnais was an active member of the Girondist party, of which Madame Roland was the soul, and he perished with them. Many of the Girondists sought safety in concealment and retreat. M. Beauharnais, conscious of his political integrity, proudly refused to save his life by turning his back upon his foes.

One morning Josephine was sitting in her parlor, in a state of great anxiety in reference to the fearful commotion of the times, when a servant announced that some one wished to speak to her. A young man of very gentle and prepossessing appearance was introduced, with a bag in his hand, in which were several pairs of shoes.

"Citizen," said the man to Josephine, "I understand that you want socks of plum gray."

The Warning.

Josephine looked up in surprise, hardly comprehending his meaning, when he approached nearer to her, and, in an under tone, whispered, "I have something to impart to you, madame."

"Explain yourself," she eagerly replied, much alarmed; "my servant is faithful."

"Ah!" he exclaimed, "my life is at stake in this matter."

"Go, Victorine," said Josephine to her servant, "and call my husband."

As soon as they were alone, the young man said, "There is not a moment to lose if you would save M. Beauharnais. The Revolutionary Committee last night passed a resolution to have him arrested, and at this very moment the warrant is making out."

"How know you this?" she demanded, trembling violently.

"I am one of the committee," was the reply, "and, being a shoemaker, I thought these shoes would afford me a reasonable pretext for advertising you, madame."

At this moment M. Beauharnais entered the room, and Josephine, weeping, threw herself into his arms. "You see my husband," she said to the shoemaker.

"I have the honor of knowing him," was the reply.

M. Beauharnais wished to reward the young man on the spot for his magnanimous and perilous deed of kindness. The offer was respectfully but decisively declined. To the earnest entreaties of Josephine and the young man that he should immediately secure his safety by his flight or concealment, he replied,

"I will never flee; with what can they charge me? I love liberty. I have borne arms for the Revolution."

"But you are a noble," the young man rejoined, "and that, in the eye of the Revolutionists, is a crime—an unpardonable crime. And, moreover, they accuse you of having been a member of the Constitutional Assembly."

"That," said M. Beauharnais, "is my most honorable title to glory. Who would not be proud of having proclaimed the rights of the nation, the fall of despotism, and the reign of laws?"

"What laws!" exclaimed Josephine. "It is in blood they are written."

"Madame," exclaimed the philanthropic young Jacobin, with a tone of severity, "when the tree of liberty is planted in an unfriendly soil, it must be watered with the blood of its enemies." Then, turning to M. Beauharnais, he said, "Within an hour it will no longer be possible to escape. I wished to save you, because I believe you innocent. Such was my duty to humanity. But if I am commanded to arrest you—pardon me—I shall do my duty; and you will acknowledge the patriot."

The young shoemaker withdrew, and Josephine in vain entreated her husband to attempt his escape. "Whither shall I flee?" he answered. "Is there a vault, a garret, a hiding-place into which the eye of the tyrant Robespierre does not penetrate? We must yield. If I am condemned, how can I escape? If I am not condemned, I have nothing to fear."

About two hours elapsed when three members of the Revolutionary Committee, accompanied by a band of armed men, broke into the house. The young shoemaker was one of this committee, and with firmness, but with much urbanity, he arrested M. Beauharnais. Josephine, as her husband was led to prison, was left in her desolated home. And she found herself indeed deserted and alone. No one could then manifest any sympathy with the proscribed without periling life. Josephine's friends, one by one, all abandoned her. The young shoemaker alone, who had arrested her husband, continued secretly to call with words of sympathy.

Josephine made great exertions to obtain the release of her husband, and was also unwearied in her benefactions to multitudes around her who, in those days of lawlessness and of anguish, were deprived of property, of friends, and of home. The only solace she found in her own grief was in ministering to the consolation of others. Josephine, from the kindest of motives, but very injudiciously, deceived her children in reference to their father's arrest, and led them to suppose that he was absent from home in consequence of ill health. When at last she obtained permission to visit, with her children, her husband in prison, they detected the deceit. After returning from the prison after their first interview, Hortense remarked to her mother that she thought her father's apartment very small, and the patients very numerous. She appeared for a time very thoughtful, and then inquired of Eugene, with an anxious expression of countenance,

"Do *you* believe that papa is ill? If he is, it certainly is not the sickness which the doctors cure."

"What do you mean, my dear child?" asked Josephine. "Can you suppose that papa and I would contrive between us to deceive you?"

"Pardon me, mamma, but I do think so."

"Why, sister," exclaimed Eugene, "how can you say so?"

"Good parents," she replied, "are unquestionably permitted to deceive their children when they wish to spare them uneasiness. Is it not so, mamma?"

Josephine was not a little embarrassed by this detection, and was compelled to acknowledge that which it was no longer possible to conceal.

In the interview which M. Beauharnais held with his wife and his children, he spoke with some freedom to his children of the injustice of his imprisonment. This sealed his doom. Listeners, who were placed in an adjoining room to note down his words, reported the conversation, and magnified it into a conspiracy for the overthrow of the republic. M. Beauharnais was immediately placed in close confinement. Josephine herself was arrested and plunged into prison, and even the terrified children were rigidly examined by a brutal committee, who, by promises and by threats, did what they could to extort from them some confession which would lead to the conviction of their parents.

Josephine, the morning of her arrest, received an anonymous letter, warning her of her danger. It was at an early hour, and her children were asleep in their beds. But how could she escape? Where could she go? Should she leave her children behind her—a mother abandon her children! Should she take them with her, and thus prevent the possibility of eluding arrest? Would not her attempt at flight be construed into a confession of guilt, and thus compromise the safety of her husband? While distracted with these thoughts, she heard a loud knocking and clamor at the outer door of the house. She understood too well the significance of those sounds. With a great effort to retain a tranquil spirit, she passed into the room where her children were sleeping. As she fixed her eyes upon them, so sweetly lost in slumber, and thought of the utter abandonment to which they were doomed, her heart throbbed with anguish, and tears, of such bitterness as are seldom shed upon earth, filled her eyes. She bent over her daughter, and imprinted a mother's farewell kiss upon her forehead. The affectionate child, though asleep, clasped her arms around her mother's neck, and, speaking the thoughts of the dream passing through her mind, said "Come to bed. Fear nothing. They shall not take you away this night. I have prayed to God for you."

The tumult in the outer hall continually increasing, Josephine, fearful of awaking Hortense and Eugene, cast a last lingering look of love upon them, and, withdrawing from the chamber, closed the door and entered her parlor. There she found a band of armed men, headed by the brutal wretch who had so unfeelingly examined her children. The soldiers were hardened against every appeal of humanity, and performed their unfeeling office without any emotion, save that of hatred for one whom they deemed to be an aristocrat. They seized Josephine rudely, and took possession of all the property in the house in the name of the Republic. They dragged their victim to the convent of the Carmelites, and she was immured in that prison, where, but a few months before, more than eight thousand had been massacred by the mob of Paris. Even the blackest annals of religious fanaticism can record no outrages more horrible than those which rampant infidelity perpetrated in these days of its temporary triumphs.

When Eugene and Hortense awoke, they found themselves indeed alone in the wide world. They were informed by a servant of the arrest and the imprisonment of their mother. The times had long been so troubled, and the children were so familiar with the recital of such scenes of violence, that they were prepared to meet these fearful perplexities with no little degree of discretion. After a few tears, they tried to summon resolution to act worthily of their father and mother. Hortense, with that energy of character which she manifested through her whole life, advised that they should go to the Luxembourg, where their father was confined, and demand admission to share his imprisonment. Eugene, with that caution which characterized him when one of the leaders in the army of Napoleon, and when viceroy of Italy, apprehensive lest thus they might in some way compromise the safety of their father, recalled to mind an aged great-aunt, who was residing in much retirement in the vicinity of Versailles, and suggested the propriety of seeking a refuge with her. An humble female friend conducted the children to Versailles, where they were most kindly received.

When the gloom of the ensuing night darkened the city, M. Beauharnais in his cheerless cell, and Josephine in her prison still stained with the blood of massacre, wept over the desolation of their home and their hopes. They knew not the fate of their children, and their minds were oppressed with the most gloomy forebodings. On the ensuing day, Josephine's heart was cheered with the tidings of their safety. Such was the second terrific storm which Josephine encountered on life's dark waters.

4

Scenes in Prison

A.D. 1794

The Convent of the Carmelites, in which Josephine was imprisoned, had acquired a fearful celebrity during the Reign of Terror. It was a vast and gloomy pile, so capacious in its halls, its chapel, its cells, and its subterranean dungeons, that at one time nearly ten thousand prisoners were immured within its frowning walls. In every part of the building the floors were still deeply stained with the blood of the recent massacres. The infuriated men and women, intoxicated with rum and rage, who had broken into the prison, dragged multitudes of their victims, many of whom were priests, into the chapel, that they might, in derision of religion, poniard them before the altar. About three hundred thousand innocent victims of the Revolution now crowded the prisons of France. These unhappy captives, awaiting the hour of their execution, were not the ignorant, the debased, the degraded, but the noblest, the purest, the most refined of the citizens of the republic. Josephine was placed in the chapel of the convent, where she found one hundred and sixty men and women as the sharers of her captivity.

The natural buoyancy of her disposition led her to take as cheerful a view as possible of the calamity in which the family was involved. Being confident that no serious charge could be brought against her husband,

THE HISTORY OF JOSEPHINE

she clung to the hope that they both would soon be liberated, and that happy days were again to dawn upon her reunited household. She wrote cheering letters to her husband and to her children. Her smiling countenance and words of kindness animated with new courage the grief-stricken and the despairing who surrounded her. She immediately became a universal favorite with the inmates of the prison. Her instinctive tact enabled her to approach all acceptably, whatever their rank or character. She soon became prominent in influence among the prisoners, and reigned there, as every where else, over the hearts of willing subjects. Her composure, her cheerfulness, her clear and melodious voice, caused her to be selected to read, each day, to the ladies, the journal of the preceding day. From their windows they could see, each morning, the carts bearing through the streets their burden of unhappy victims who were to perish on the scaffold. Not unfrequently a wife would catch a glimpse of her husband, or a mother of her son, borne past the grated windows in the cart of the condemned. Who can tell the fear and anguish with which the catalogue of the guillotined was read, when each trembling heart apprehended that the next word might announce that some loved one had perished? Not unfrequently a piercing shriek, and a fainting form falling lifeless upon the floor, revealed upon whose heart the blow had fallen.

Hortense, impetuous and unreflecting, was so impatient to see her mother, that one morning she secretly left her aunt's house, and, in a market cart, traveled thirty miles to Paris. She found her mother's maid, Victorine, at the family mansion, where all the property was sealed up by the revolutionary functionaries. After making unavailing efforts to obtain an interview with her parents, she returned the next day to Fontainebleau. Josephine was informed of this imprudent act of ardent affection, and wrote to her child the following admirable letter:

> "I should be entirely satisfied with the good heart of my Hortense were I not displeased with her bad head. How is it, my daughter, that, without permission from your aunt, you have come to

Paris? This was very wrong! But it was to see me, you will say. You ought to be aware that no one can see me without an order, to obtain which requires both means and precautions. And, besides, you got upon M. Dorcet's cart, at the risk of incommoding him and retarding the conveyance of his merchandise. In all this you have been very inconsiderate. My child! observe, it is not sufficient to do good; you must also do good properly. At your age, the first of all virtues is confidence and docility toward your relations. I am therefore obliged to tell you that I prefer your tranquil attachment to your misplaced warmth. This, however, does not prevent me from embracing you, but less tenderly than I shall do when I learn that you have returned to your aunt."

There was at this time, for some unknown reason, a little mitigation in the severity with which the prisoners were treated, and Josephine was very sanguine in the belief that the hour of their release was at hand. Emboldened by this hope, she wrote a very earnest appeal to the Committee of Public Safety, before whom the accusations against M. Beauharnais would be brought. The sincerity and frankness of the eloquent address so touched the feelings of the president of the committee, that he resolved to secure for Josephine and her husband the indulgence of an interview. The greatest caution was necessary in doing this, for he periled his own life by the manifestation of any sympathy for the accused.

The only way in which he could accomplish his benevolent project was to have them both brought together for trial. Neither of them knew of this design. One morning Josephine, while dreaming of liberty and of her children, was startled by the unexpected summons to appear before the Revolutionary tribunal. She knew that justice had no voice which could be heard before that merciless and sanguinary court. She knew that the mockery of a trial was but the precursor of the sentence, which was immediately followed by the execution. From her high hopes this summons caused a fearful fall. Thoughts of her husband and her children rushed in upon her overflowing heart, and the tenderness of the woman for a few moments triumphed over the heroine. Soon, however, regaining in some degree her composure, she prepared herself, with as much calmness as possible, to meet her doom. She was led from her prison to the hall where the blood-stained tribunal held its session, and, with many others, was placed in an ante-room, to await her turn for an examination of a few minutes, upon the issues of which life or death was suspended. While Josephine was sitting here, in the anguish of suspense, an opposite door was opened, and some armed soldiers led in a group of victims from another prison. As Josephine's eye vacantly wandered over their features, she was startled by the entrance of one whose wan and haggard features strikingly reminded her of her husband. She looked again, their eyes met, and husband and wife were instantly locked in each other's embrace. At this interview, the stoicism of M. Beauharnais was entirely subdued—the thoughts of the past, of his unworthiness, of the faithful and generous love of Josephine, rushed in a resistless flood upon his soul. He leaned his aching head upon the forgiving bosom of Josephine, and surrendered himself to love, and penitence, and tears.

This brief and painful interview was their last. They never met again. They were allowed but a few moments together ere the officers came and dragged M. Beauharnais before the judges. His examination lasted but a few minutes, when he was remanded back to prison. Nothing was proved against him. No serious accusation even was laid to his charge. But he was a noble. He had descended from illustrious ancestors, and therefore, as an aristocrat, he was doomed to die. Josephine was also conducted into the presence of this sanguinary tribunal. She was the wife of a nobleman. She was the friend of Marie Antoinette. She had even received distinguished attentions at court. These crimes consigned her also to the guillotine. Josephine was conducted back to her prison, unconscious of the sentence which had been pronounced against her husband and herself. She even cherished the sanguine hope that they would soon be liberated, for she could not think it possible that they could be doomed to death without even the accusation of crime.

Each evening there was brought into the prison a list of the names of those who were to be led to the guillotine on the ensuing morning. A few days after the trial, on the evening of the 24th of July, 1794, M. Beauharnais found his name with the proscribed who were to be led to the scaffold with the light of the next day. Love for his wife and his children rendered life too precious to him to be surrendered without anguish. But sorrow had subdued his heart, and led him with prayerfulness to look to God for strength to meet the trial. The native dignity of his character also nerved him to meet his fate with fortitude.

He sat down calmly in his cell, and wrote a long, affectionate, and touching letter to his wife. He assured her of his most heartfelt appreciation of the purity and nobleness of her character, and of her priceless worth as a wife and a mother. He thanked her again and again for the generous spirit with which she forgave his offenses, when, weary and contrite, he returned from his guilty wanderings, and anew sought her love. He implored her to cherish in the hearts of his children the memory of their father, that, though dead, he might still live in their affections. While he was writing, the executioners came in to cut off his long hair, that the ax might do its work unimpeded. Picking up a small lock from the floor, he wished to transmit it to his wife as his last legacy. The brutal executioners forbade him the privilege. He, however, succeeded in purchasing from them a few hairs, which he inclosed in his letter, and which she subsequently received.

In the early dawn of the morning, the cart of the condemned was at the prison door. The Parisians were beginning to be weary of the abundant flow of blood, and Robespierre had therefore caused the guillotine to be removed from the Place de la Revolution to an obscure spot in the Faubourg St. Antoine. A large number of victims were doomed to die that morning. The carts, as they rolled along the pavements, groaned with their burdens, and the persons in the streets looked on in sullen silence. M. Beauharnais, with firmness, ascended the scaffold. The slide of the guillotine fell, and the brief drama of his stormy life was ended.

While the mutilated form of M. Beauharnais was borne to an ignoble burial, Josephine, entirely unconscious of the calamity which had befallen her, was cheering her heart with the hope of a speedy union with her husband and her children in their own loved home. The morning after the execution, the daily journal, containing the names of those who had perished on the preceding day, was brought, as usual, to the prison. Some of the ladies in the prison had received the intimation that M. Beauharnais had fallen. They watched, therefore, the arrival of the journal, and, finding their fears established, they tried, for a time, to conceal the dreadful intelligence from the unconscious widow. But Josephine was eagerly inquiring for the paper, and at last obtaining it, she ran her eye hastily over the record of executions, and found the name of her husband in the fatal list. She fell senseless upon the floor. For a long time she remained in a swoon. When consciousness returned, and with it a sense of the misery into which she was plunged, in the delirium of her anguish she exclaimed, "Oh God! let me die! let me die! There is no peace for me but in the grave."

Her friends gathered around her. They implored her to think of her children, and for their sake to prize a life she could no longer prize for her own. The poignancy of her grief gradually subsided into the calm of despair. A sleepless night lingered slowly away. The darkness and the gloom of a prison settled down upon her soul. The morning dawned drearily. A band of rough and merciless agents from the Revolutionary Assembly came to her with the almost welcome intelligence that in two days she was to be led to the Conciergerie, and from thence to her execution. These tidings would have been joyful to Josephine were it not for her children. A mother's love clung to the orphans, and it was with pain inexpressible that she thought of leaving them alone in this tempestuous world—a world made so stormy, so woeful, by man's inhumanity to his fellow-man.

The day preceding the one assigned for her execution arrived. The numerous friends of Josephine in the prison hung around her with tears. The heartless jailer came and took away her mattress, saying, with a sneer, that she would need it no longer, as her head was soon to repose upon the soft pillow of the guillotine. It is reported that, as the hour of execution drew nearer, Josephine became not only perfectly calm, but even cheerful in spirit. She looked affectionately upon the weeping group gathered around her, and, recalling at the moment the prediction of the aged negress, gently smiling, said, "We have no cause for alarm my friends; I am not to be executed. It is written in the decrees of Fate that I am yet to be Queen of France." Some of her friends thought that the suppressed anguish of her heart had driven her to delirium, and they wept more bitterly. But one of the ladies, Madame d'Aiguillon, was a little irritated at pleasantry which she deemed so ill timed. With something like resentment, she asked, "Why, then, madame, do you not appoint your household?" "Ah! that is true," Josephine replied. "I had forgotten. Well, you, my dear, shall be my maid of honor. I promise you the situation." They both lived to witness the strange fulfillment of this promise. Josephine, however, who, from the circumstances of her early life, was inclined to credulity, afterward declared that at the time her mind reposed in the full confidence that in some way her life would be saved, and that the prediction of the negress would be virtually realized.

The shades of night settled down around the gloomy convent, enveloping in their folds the despairing hearts which thronged this abode of woe. Suddenly the most exultant shout of joy burst from every lip, and echoed along through corridors, and dungeons, and grated cells. There was weeping and fainting for rapture inexpressible. The prisoners leaped into each other's arms, and, frantic with happiness, clung together in that long and heartfelt embrace which none can appreciate but those who have been companions in woe. Into the blackness of their midnight there had suddenly burst the blaze of noonday. What caused this apparently miraculous change? The iron-hearted jailer had passed along, announcing, in coarsest phrase, that Robespierre was guillotined. There had been a new revolution. The tyrant had fallen. The prisons which he had filled with victims were to be emptied of their captives.

5

The Release from Prison

A.D. 1794-A.D. 1795

The overthrow of Robespierre, and the consequent escape of Josephine from the doom impending over her, was in the following manner most strangely accomplished. The tyranny of Robespierre had become nearly insupportable. Conspiracies were beginning to be formed to attempt his overthrow. A lady of great beauty and celebrity, Madame de Fontenay, was imprisoned with Josephine. M. Tallien, a man of much influence with a new party then rising into power, had conceived a strong attachment for this lady, and, though he could not safely indulge himself in interviews with her in prison, he was in the habit of coming daily to the Convent of the Carmelites that he might have the satisfaction of catching a glimpse of the one he loved through her grated window.

Madame de Fontenay had received secret intelligence that she was soon to be led before the Convention for trial. This she knew to be but the prelude of her execution. That evening M. Tallien appeared as usual before the guarded casement of the Carmelites. Madame de Fontenay and Josephine, arm in arm, leaned against the bars of the window, as if to breathe the fresh evening air, and made a sign to arrest M. Tallien's particular attention. They then dropped from the window a piece of cabbage-leaf, in which Madame de Fontenay had inclosed the following note:

> "My trial is decreed—the result is certain. If you love me as you say, urge every means to save France and me."

With intense interest, they watched the motions of M. Tallien until they saw him take the cabbage-leaf from the ground. Roused by the billet to the consciousness of the necessity of immediate action, he proceeded to the Convention, and, with the impassioned energy which love for Madame de Fontenay and hatred of Robespierre inspired, made an energetic and fearless assault upon the tyrant. Robespierre, pale and trembling, saw that his hour had come. A decree of accusation was preferred against him, and the head of the merciless despot fell upon that guillotine where he had already caused so many thousands to perish. The day before Josephine was to have been executed, he was led, mangled and bleeding, to the scaffold. He had attempted to commit suicide. The ball missed its aim, but shattered his jaw. The wretched man ascended the ladder, and stood upon the platform of the guillotine. The executioners tore the bandage from his mangled face, that the linen might not impede the blow of the ax. Their rude treatment of the inflamed wound extorted a cry of agony, which thrilled upon the ear of the assembled crowd, and produced a silence as of the grave. The next moment the slide fell, and the mutilated head was severed from the body. Then the very heavens seemed rent by one long, loud, exulting shout, which proclaimed that Robespierre was no more!

The death of Robespierre arrested the ax which was just about to fall upon the head of Josephine. The first intimation of his overthrow was communicated to her in the following singular manner. Madame d'Aiguillon was weeping bitterly, and sinking down with faintness in view of the bloody death to which her friend was to be led on the morrow. Josephine, whose fortitude had not forsaken her, drew her almost senseless companion to the window, that she might be revived by the fresh lair. Her attention was arrested by a woman of the lower orders in the street, who was continually looking up to the window, beckoning to Josephine, and making many very singular gestures. She seemed to desire to call her attention particularly to the *robe* which she wore, holding it up, and pointing to it again and again. Josephine, through the iron grating, cried out *Robe*. The woman eagerly gave signs of assent, and immediately took up a stone, which in French is *Pierre*. Josephine again cried out *pierre*. The woman appeared overjoyed on perceiving that her pantomime began to be understood. She then put the two together, pointing alternately to the one and to the other. Josephine cried out *Robespierre*. The woman then began to dance and shout with delight, and made signs of cutting off a head.

The Pantomime.

This pantomime excited emotions in the bosom of Josephine which cannot be described. She hardly dared to believe that the tyrant had actually fallen, and yet she knew not how else to account for the singular conduct of the woman. But a few moments elapsed before a great noise was heard in the corridor of the prison. The turnkey, in loud and fearless tones, cried out to his dog, "Get out, you cursed brute of a Robespierre!" This emphatic phraseology convinced them that the sanguinary monster before whom all France had trembled was no longer to be feared. In a few moments the glad tidings were resounding through the prison, and many were in an instant raised from the abyss of despair to almost a delirium of bliss. Josephine's bed was restored to her, and she placed her head upon her pillow that night, and sank down to the most calm and delightful repose.

No language can describe the transports excited throughout all France by the tidings of the fall of Robespierre. Three hundred thousand captives were then lingering in the prisons of Paris awaiting death. As the glittering steel severed the head of the tyrant from his body, their prison doors burst open, and France was filled with hearts throbbing with ecstasy, and with eyes overflowing with tears of rapture. Five hundred thousand fugitives were trembling in their retreats, apprehensive of arrest. They issued from their hiding-places frantic with joy, and every village witnessed their tears and embraces.

The new party which now came into power with Tallien at its head, immediately liberated those who had been condemned by their opponents, and the prison doors of Josephine were thrown open to her. But from the gloom of her cell she returned to a world still dark and clouded. Her husband had been beheaded, and all his property confiscated. She found herself a widow and penniless. Nearly all of her friends had perished in the storms which had swept over France. The Reign of Terror had passed away, but gaunt famine was staring the nation in the face. They were moments of ecstasy when Josephine, again free, pressed Eugene and Hortense to her heart. But the most serious embarrassments immediately crowded upon her. Poverty, stern and apparently remediless, was her lot. She had no friends upon whom she had any right to call for aid. There was no employment open before her by which she could obtain her subsistence; and it appeared that she and her children were to be reduced to absolute beggary. These were among the darkest hours of her earthly career. It was from this abyss of obscurity and want that she was to be raised to a position of splendor and of power such as the wildest dreams of earthly ambition could hardly have conceived.

Though Robespierre was dead, the strife of rancorous parties raged with unabated violence, and blood flowed freely. The reign of the mob still continued, and it was a mark of patriotism demanded by the clamors of haggard want and degradation to persecute all of noble blood. Young girls from the boarding-schools, and boys just emerging from the period of childhood, were beheaded by the guillotine. "We must exterminate," said Marat, "all the *whelps* of aristocracy." Josephine trembled for her children. Poverty, and the desire of concealing Eugene among the mass of the people, induced her to apprentice her son to a house-carpenter. For several months Eugene cheerfully and laboriously toiled in this humble occupation. But the sentiments he had imbibed from both father and mother ennobled him, and every day produced new developments of a lofty character, which no circumstances could long depress.

Let such a woman as Josephine, with her cheerful, magnanimous, self-sacrificing, and generous spirit, be left destitute in any place where human beings are congregated, and she will soon inevitably meet with those who will feel honored in securing her friendship and in offering her a home. Every fireside has a welcome for a noble heart. Madame Dumoulin, a lady of great elevation of character, whose large fortune had by some chance escaped the general wreck, invited Josephine to her house, and freely supplied her wants. Madame Fontenay, also, who was a woman of great beauty and accomplishments, soon after her liberation was married to M. Tallien, to whom she had tossed the note, inclosed in a cabbage-leaf, from her prison window. It was this note which had so suddenly secured the overthrow of the tyrant, and had rescued so many from the guillotine. They both became the firm friends of Josephine. Others, also, soon became strongly attracted to her by the loveliness of her character, and were ambitious to supply all her wants.

Through M. Tallien, she urged her claim upon the National Convention for the restoration of her confiscated property. After a long and tedious process, she succeeded in regaining such a portion of her estate as to provide her amply with all the comforts of life. Again she had her own peaceful home, with Eugene and Hortense by her side. Her natural buoyancy of spirits rose superior to the storms which had swept so mercilessly over her, and in the love of her idolized children, and surrounded by the sympathies of appreciative friends, days of serenity, and even of joy, began to shine upon her.

A domestic scene occurred in the dwelling of Josephine on the anniversary of the death of M. Beauharnais peculiarly characteristic of the times and of the French people. Josephine called Eugene to her room, and presented to him a portrait of his father. "Carry it to your chamber, my son," she said, "and often let it be the object of your contemplations. Above all, let him whose image it presents be your constant model. He was the most amiable of men; he would have been the best of fathers."

Eugene was a young man of that enthusiastic genius which is the almost invariable accompaniment of a noble character. His emotions were deeply excited. With the characteristic ardor of his countrymen, he covered the portrait with kisses, and wept freely. Josephine folded her noble boy in her embrace, and they mingled their tears together.

In the evening, as Josephine was sitting alone in her parlor, her son entered, accompanied by six young men, his companions, each decorated with a copy of the portrait of M. Beauharnais suspended from the neck by a black and white ribbon. "You see," said Eugene to his mother, "the founders of a new order of knighthood. Behold our tutelary saint," pointing to the portrait of his father. "And these are the first members." He then introduced his youthful companions to his mother.

"Ours," he continued, "is named the Order of *Filial Love*; and, if you would witness the first inauguration, pass with these gentlemen into the small drawing-room."

Josephine entered the drawing-room with the youthful group, and found it very tastefully ornamented with garlands of ivy, roses, and laurels. Inscriptions, taken from the printed discourses or remarkable sayings of M. Beauharnais, were suspended upon the walls. Girandoles, with lighted tapers, brilliantly illuminated the room. An altar was erected, hung with festoons of flowers, and upon this altar was placed the full-length portrait of M. Beauharnais. Three crowns of white and red roses were suspended from the picture-frame, and in front were placed two vases with perfumes.

The young gentlemen ranged themselves about the altar in perfect silence, and, at a concerted signal, eagerly unsheathed the swords which they wore at their sides, and, clasping hands, solemnly took the oath, *"To love their parents, succor each other, and to defend their country."* At this moment, Eugene, unfurling and waving a small banner, with its folds shaded the head of his father. "We then embraced each other," says Josephine, "mingling tears with smiles, and the most amiable disorder succeeded to the ceremonial of inauguration."

The fascination of Josephine's person and address drew multitudes of friends around her, and her society was ever coveted. As time softened the poignancy of her past sorrows, she mingled more and more in the social circles of that metropolis where pleasure and gayety ever reign. The terrible convulsions of the times had thrown the whole fabric of society into confusion. Great efforts were now made to revive the festivities of former days. Two centers of society were naturally established. The first included that in which Josephine moved. It was composed of the remains of the ancient nobility, who had returned to Paris with the fragments of their families and their shattered fortunes. Rigid economy was necessary to keep up any appearance of elegance. But that polish of manners which almost invariably descends from an illustrious ancestry marked all their intercourse. The humiliations through which the nobles had passed had not diminished the exclusiveness of their tastes. The other circle was composed of merchants and bankers who had acquired opulence in the midst of the confiscations and storms of revolution. The passion for display was prominent in all their assemblies, as is necessarily the case with those whose passport to distinction is wealth.

At the theaters and all the places of public festivity, there were presented studied memorials of the scenes of horror through which all had recently passed. One of the most fashionable and brilliant assemblies then known in Paris was called *The Ball of the Victims*. No one was admitted to this assembly who had not lost some near relative by the guillotine. The most fashionable style of dressing the hair was jocosely called "à la guillotine." The hair was arranged in the manner in which it had been adjusted by the executioner for the unimpeded operation of the ax. And thus, with songs, and dances, and laughter-moving jokes, they commemorated the bloody death of their friends.

A new insurrection by the populace of Paris was at this time planned against the Convention. The exasperated people were again to march upon the Tuilleries. The members were in extreme consternation. The mob could bring tens of thousands against them, well armed with muskets and heavy artillery. There were but five hundred regular troops with which to resist the onset. Menou, the officer in command, acknowledged his inability to meet the crisis, and surrendered his power to Barras. This general immediately, as by a sudden thought, exclaimed, "I know the man who can defend us! He is a little Corsican, who dares do any thing, and is perfectly reckless of consequences!"

The little Corsican, Napoleon Bonaparte, the day-star of whose fame was just beginning to rise over the smouldering ruins of Toulon, was invited to meet the Convention. His fragile form was almost feminine in its proportions, but an eagle eye calmly reposed in his pallid and emaciate countenance. He had been severely sick, and the Convention looked with amazement and incredulity upon this feeble youth, as the one presented to rescue them from their impending peril.

The president fixed his eye upon him doubtingly, and said, "Are you willing to undertake our defense?"

"Yes!" was the calm, laconic, and almost indifferent reply.

"But are you aware of the magnitude of the undertaking?"

"Fully!" said Napoleon, fixing his piercing eye upon the president; "and I am in the habit of accomplishing that which I undertake."

From that moment his authority was established. Every member of the Convention felt the mysterious fascination of his master mind. Barras surrendered the whole command into his hands. He instantly called into the city all the national forces which were around Paris, and disposed fifty pieces of heavy artillery, under the command of Murat, so as to rake all the avenues to the Convention. His calm and almost superhuman energy sought no repose that night. The delay of but a few moments would have placed this very park of artillery, which secured his victory, in the hands of the insurgents. When the morning dawned, the Tuilleries, as if by magic, had assumed the aspect of a fortified camp. The little Corsican was silently and calmly awaiting the onset, as secure of triumph as if the victory were already achieved.

But in every quarter of Paris, during the night, the insurgents had been mustering their forces, and the mutterings of the approaching storm were dismally echoed through the streets of the metropolis. Above thirty thousand men, all well armed with musketry and artillery, in regular military array, and under experienced generals, came pouring down upon the feeble band which surrounded the Convention.

Will the little Corsican dare to fire upon the people? Will this pale and slender youth, who had hardly yet entered upon the period of manhood, dare to deluge the pavements of Paris with the blood of her own citizens? Will he venture upon a conflict so unequal, when failure is his certain death?

Napoleon, with his colorless cheek, his flashing eye, and his air of mysterious melancholy, stood in silence, as the gathering thousands crowded down upon him. He offered no parley; he uttered not a word of warning; he condescended to no threats. The insurgents, believing that he would not dare to fire upon them, advanced within fifty yards of his masked battery, when he opened his columns, and, in the roar of artillery shotted to the muzzle, the voice of Napoleon was for the first time heard in the streets of Paris. The thunder of his tones was preceded by the lightning's bolt. The merciless storm of grape-shot, sweeping the streets, covered the ground with the dead and the dying. No mortal could withstand such a conflict. The advancing foe wavered for an instant, and then, in the utmost consternation, took to flight. Napoleon commanded immediately the most rapid discharge of blank cartridges.

Peal upon peal, their loud reverberations deafened the city, and added wings to the flight of the terror-stricken crowd. But a few moments elapsed ere not even a straggler could be seen in the deserted streets. The little Corsican, pale and calm, stood, with folded arms, as unperturbed as if no event of any moment had occurred. During the whole day, however, the conflict continued in different parts of the city, but before nightfall the insurgents were every where entirely discomfited.

Paris was now filled with the name of Napoleon. Some regarded him as a savior, protecting the Convention; others considered him a demon, deluging the capital with blood. One evening, Josephine was visiting at the house of a friend, and sitting by a window examining some beautiful violets, when *Bonaparte* was announced. Josephine had never yet met him, though, of course, she had heard much of one whose rising fame filled the metropolis.

She says that she trembled violently at the announcement of his name. His entrance seemed to excite general interest, and all eyes were turned toward him, though most of the company regarded him in silence. He approached Josephine, and the subject of the recent conflict in the streets of Paris was introduced.

"It seems to me," said Josephine, "that it is only with regret that we should think of the consternation you have spread through the capital. It is a frightful service you have performed."

"It is very possible," he replied. "The military are only automata, to which the government gives such motions as it pleases. They have no duty but to obey. Besides, I wished to teach the Parisians a little lesson. *This is my seal which I have set upon France.*"

This he said in such calm, quiet, imperturbable tones, so expressive of his perfect confidence in himself, and of his indifference to the opinions of others, that Josephine was quite piqued, and replied politely, but yet in a manner which indicated her displeasure.

"These light skirmishes," the young general rejoined, "are but the first coruscations of my glory."

"If you are to acquire glory at such a price," Josephine answered, "I would much rather count you among the victims."

Such was the first interview between Josephine and Napoleon. It was merely a casual meeting in an evening party between a widow, graceful and beautiful, and a young man of boundless ambition. Though Josephine was not pleased with Napoleon, he produced a very profound impression upon her mind. Napoleon, being now in command of the troops in Paris, by order of the Convention, executed the very unpopular office of disarming the populace. In the performance of this order, the sword of M. Beauharnais was taken. The next day, Eugene, who was then a boy twelve years of age, of exceedingly prepossessing appearance, presented himself before Napoleon, and implored the return of the sword which had belonged to his father. Napoleon was deeply interested in the frankness and the fervor of emotion manifested by the lad, and immediately complied with his request. Josephine called upon him the next day to thank him for his kindness to her son. He was at this interview as deeply impressed by the fascinations of the mother as he had previously been struck by the noble bearing of the child. After this they frequently met, and Josephine could not be blind to the interest with which she was regarded by Napoleon. Situated as he then was, it was social elevation to him to be united with Madame de Beauharnais, and her rank, and influence, and troops of friends would greatly aid him in his ambitious plans. It is also unquestionably true that Napoleon formed a very strong attachment for Josephine. Indeed, she was the only person whom he ever truly loved. That he did love her at times most passionately there can be no doubt.

Josephine, however, had many misgivings respecting the expediency of the union. She stated to her friends that he was the most fascinating man that she had ever met; that she admired his courage, the quickness of his judgment, the extent of his information. She, however, confessed that she did not really love him—that she stood in awe of him. "His searching glance," she says, "mysterious and inexplicable, imposes even upon our Directors—judge if it may not intimidate a woman."

"Being now past the heyday of youth," she writes in a letter to a friend, "can I hope long to preserve that ardor of attachment which, in the general, resembles a fit of delirium? If, after our union, he should cease to love me, will he not reproach me with what he will have sacrificed for my sake? Will he not regret a more brilliant marriage which he might have contracted? What shall I then reply? What shall I do? I shall weep. Excellent resource! you will say. Alas! I know that all this can serve no end; but it has ever been thus; tears are the only resource left me when this poor heart, so easily chilled, has suffered. Write quickly, and do not fear to scold me, should you judge that I am wrong. You know that whatever comes from your pen will be taken in good part.

"Barras gives assurance that if I marry the general, he will so contrive as to have him appointed to the command of the army of Italy. Yesterday, Bonaparte, speaking of this favor, which already excites murmuring among his fellow-soldiers, though it be as yet only a promise, said to me, 'Think they, then, I have need of their protection to arrive at power? Egregious mistake! They will all be but too happy one day should I grant them mine. My sword is by my side, and with it I will go far.'

"What say you to this security of success? Is it not a proof of confidence springing from an excess of vanity? A general of brigade protect the heads of government! that, truly, is an event highly probable! I know not how it is, but sometimes this waywardness gains upon me to such a degree that almost I believe possible whatever this singular man may take it in his head to attempt; and, with his imagination, who can calculate what he will not undertake?"

It was now winter. The storm of Revolution had partially subsided. The times were, however, full of agitation and peril. Europe was in arms against France. There was no stable government and no respected laws. The ambitious young general consecrated his days with sleepless energy to his public duties, but each evening he devoted to Josephine. Napoleon never manifested any taste for those dissipating pleasures which attract and ruin so many young men. He had no moral principles which pronounced such indulgences wrong, but the grandeur of his ambition absorbed all his energies. He was, even at that time, a hard student. He was never more happy than when alone with Josephine, engaged in conversation or reading. His attachment for Josephine became very ardent and passionate. The female character at this time, in France, was far from high. Napoleon had but little respect for ladies in general. The circumstances of his life had led him to form a low estimate of the sex. He often said that all the rest of the sex were nothing compared with Josephine. He frequently gave public breakfasts to his friends, at which Josephine universally presided, though other ladies were invited.

In the pleasant mansion of Josephine, Napoleon was in the habit of meeting a small circle of select friends, who were strongly attached to Josephine, and who were able, and for her sake were willing to promote his interests. Napoleon was a man of strong affections, but of stronger ambition. Josephine was entirely satisfied with the singleness and the ardor of his love. She sometimes trembled in view of its violence. She often remarked to her friends that he was incomparably the most fascinating man she had ever met. All have equally attested Napoleon's unrivaled powers of pleasing, whenever it suited his purpose to make the effort. The winter thus rapidly and pleasantly passed away.

6

Josephine in Italy

A.D. 1796-A.D. 1797

On the 9th of March, 1796, Josephine was married to Napoleon. The Revolution had swept away every thing that was sacred in human and divine institutions, and the attempt had been made to degrade marriage into a mere partnership, which any persons might contract or dissolve at pleasure. According to the Revolutionary form, Josephine and Napoleon presented themselves before a magistrate, and simply announced their union. A few friends attended as witnesses of the ceremony.

Napoleon had, in the mean time, been appointed commander of the French forces in Italy. In twelve days after his nuptials, he left his bride and hastened to the army, then in the lowest state of poverty and suffering. The veteran generals, when they first saw the pale-faced youth who was placed over them all, were disposed to treat him with contempt. Hardly an hour elapsed after his arrival ere they felt and admitted that he was their master. He seemed insensible to mental exhaustion, or fatigue, or hunger, or want of sleep. He was upon horseback night and day. Almost supernatural activity was infused into the army. It fell like an avalanche upon the Austrians. In fifteen days after he took command, he proclaimed to his exulting and victorious troops,

THE HISTORY OF JOSEPHINE

"Soldiers! you have gained in fifteen days six victories, taken one-and-twenty standards, fifty-five pieces of cannon, many strong places, and conquered the richest part of Piedmont; you have made fifteen thousand prisoners, and killed or wounded ten thousand men."

Paris was perfectly intoxicated with the announcement, day after day, of these brilliant achievements. The name of Napoleon was upon every lip, and all France resounded with his praises. "This young commander," said one of the discomfited veteran generals of the Austrian army, "knows nothing whatever about the art of war. He is a perfect ignoramus. He sets at defiance all the established rules of military tactics. There is no doing any thing with him."

Napoleon, after a series of terrible conflicts and most signal triumphs, drove the Austrians out of Italy, pursued them into their own country, and at Leoben, almost within sight of the steeples of Vienna, dictated a peace, which crowned him, in the estimation of his countrymen, with the highest glory. Josephine now went from Paris to Italy to meet her triumphant husband. They took up their residence at the Castle of Montebello, a most delightful country seat in the vicinity of Milan.

And here Josephine passed a few months of almost unalloyed happiness. The dark and tempestuous days through which she had recently been led, had prepared her to enjoy most exquisitely the calm which ensued. She had been in the deepest penury. She was now in the enjoyment of all that wealth could confer. She had been widowed and homeless. She was now the wife of a victorious general whose fame was reverberating through Europe, and her home combined almost every conceivable attraction. She had been a prisoner doomed to die, and her very jailer feared to speak to her in tones of kindness. Now she was caressed by nobles and princes; all the splendors of a court surrounded her, and every heart did her homage. Josephine presided at all her receptions and entertainments with an elegance of manner so winning as perfectly to fascinate the Milanese. "I conquer provinces," said Napoleon of her at that time, "but Josephine wins hearts." The vicinity of Montebello combines perhaps as much of the beautiful and the sublime in scenery as can be found at any other spot on the surface of the globe. Napoleon sympathized most cordially with Josephine in her appreciation of the beautiful and the romantic; and though he devoted the energies of his mind, with unsleeping diligence, to the ambitious plans which engrossed him, he found time for many delightful excursions with his fascinating bride. There is not, perhaps, in Italy a more lovely drive than that from Milan, along the crystal waters of Lake Como to Lake Maggiore. This romantic lake, embosomed among the mountains, with its densely wooded islands and picturesque shores, was a favorite resort for excursions of pleasure. Here, in gay parties, they floated in boats, with well-trained rowers, and silken awnings, and streaming pennants, and ravishing music. The island of Isola Bella, or *Beautiful Island*, with its arcades, its hanging gardens, and its palace of monkish gloom, was Napoleon's favorite landing-place. Here they often partook of refreshments, and engaged with all vivacity in rural festivities. It is stated that, while enjoying one of these excursions, Josephine, with one or two other ladies, was standing under a beautiful orange-tree, loaded with fruit, with the attention of the party all absorbed in admiring the beauties of the distant landscape. Napoleon, unperceived, crept up the tree, and by a sudden shake brought down quite a shower of the golden fruit upon the ladies. The companions of Josephine screamed with affright and ran from the tree. She, however, accustomed to such pleasantries, suspected the source, and remained unmoved. "Why, Josephine!" exclaimed Napoleon, "you stand fire like one of my veterans." "And why should I not?" she promptly replied, "am I not the wife of their commander?"

Napoleon, during these scenes of apparent relaxation, had but one thought—ambition. His capacious mind was ever restless, ever excited, not exactly with the desire of personal aggrandizement, but of mighty enterprise, of magnificent achievement. Josephine, with her boundless popularity and her arts of persuasion, though she often trembled in view of the limitless aspirations of her husband, was extremely influential in winning to him the powerful friends by whom they were surrounded.

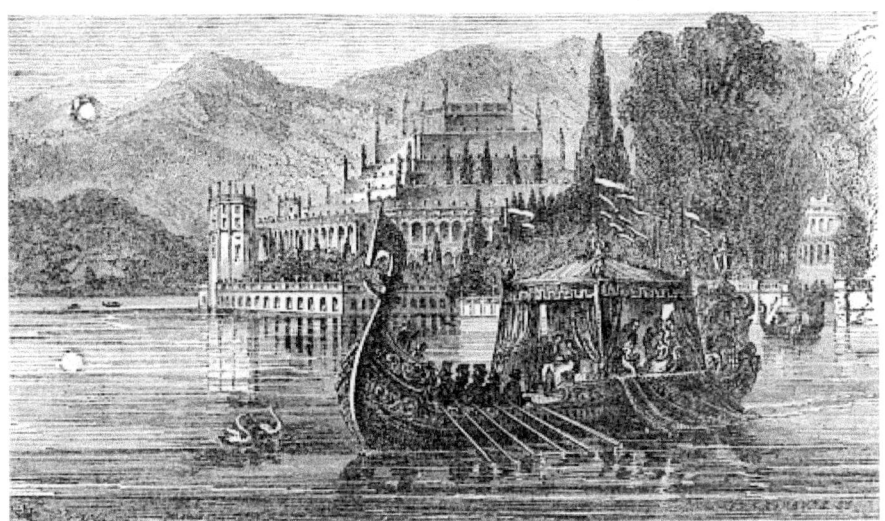

Isola Bella.

The achievements which Napoleon accomplished during the short Italian campaign are perhaps unparalleled in ancient or modern warfare.

With a number of men under his command ever inferior to the forces of the Austrians, he maneuvered always to secure, at any one point, an array superior to that of his antagonists. He cut up four several armies which were sent from Austria to oppose him, took one hundred and fifteen thousand prisoners, one hundred and seventy standards, eleven hundred and forty pieces of battering cannon and field artillery, and drove the Austrians from the frontiers of France to the walls of Vienna. He was every where hailed as the liberator of Italy; and, encircled with the pomp and the power of a monarch, he received such adulation as monarchs rarely enjoy.

The Directory in Paris began to tremble in view of the gigantic strides which this ambitious general was making. They surrounded him with spies to garner up his words, to watch his actions, and, if possible, to detect his plans. But the marble face of this incomprehensible youth told no secrets. Even to Josephine he revealed not his intentions; and no mortal scrutiny could explore the thoughts fermenting in his deep and capacious mind. His personal appearance at this time is thus described by an observer of his triumphal entrance into Milan:

> "I beheld with deep interest and extreme attention that extraordinary man who has performed such great deeds, and about whom there is something which seems to indicate that his career is not yet terminated. I found him very like his portrait, small in stature, thin, pale, with the air of fatigue, but not in ill health. He appeared to me to listen with more abstraction than interest, as if occupied rather with what he was thinking of than with what was said to him. There is great intelligence in his countenance, along with an expression of habitual meditation, which reveals nothing of what is passing within. In that thinking head, in that daring mind, it is impossible not to suppose that some designs are engendering which shall have their influence upon the destinies of Europe."

Napoleon was fully confident of the jealousy he had aroused, and of the vigilance with which he was watched. His caution often wounded Josephine, as he was as impenetrable to her in reference to all his political plans as to any one else. While she at times loved him almost to adoration, she ever felt in awe of the unexplored recesses of his mind. He appeared frequently lost in thought, and, perfectly regardless of the pomp and the pageantry with which he was surrounded, he gave unmistakable indications that he regarded the achievements he had already accomplished as very trivial—merely the commencement of his career. She once remarked to a friend, "During the many years we have now passed together, I never once beheld Bonaparte for a moment at ease—not even with myself. He is constantly on the alert. If at any time he appears to show a little confidence, it is merely a feint to throw the person with whom he is conversing off his guard, and to draw forth his real sentiments, but never does he himself disclose his own thoughts."

Napoleon now deemed it expedient to visit Paris; for he despised the weakness and the inefficiency of those who, amid the surges of the Revolution, had been elevated there to the supreme power, and already he secretly contemplated the overthrow of the government, as soon as an opportunity promising success should be presented. Josephine, with her children, remained in Milan, that she might continue to dazzle the eyes of the Milanese with the splendor of the establishment of the Liberator of Italy, and that she might watch over the interests of her illustrious spouse.

She gave splendid entertainments. Her saloons were ever thronged with courtiers, and the inimitable grace she possessed enabled her, with ease and self-enjoyment, to preside with queenly dignity over every scene of gayety. She was often weary of this incessant grandeur and display, but the wishes of her husband and her peculiar position seemed to afford her no choice. Napoleon unquestionably loved Josephine as ardently as he was capable of loving any one. He kept up a constant, almost a daily correspondence with her. Near the close of his life, he declared that he was indebted to her for every moment of happiness he had known on earth. Ambition was, however, with Napoleon a far more powerful passion than love. He was fully conscious that he needed the assistance of his most accomplished wife to raise him to that elevation he was resolved to attain. Self-reliant as he was, regardless as he ever appeared to be of the opinions or the advice of others, the counsel of Josephine had more influence over him than perhaps that of all other persons combined. Her expostulations not unfrequently modified his plans, though his high spirit could not brook the acknowledgment. Hortense and Eugene were with Josephine at Milan. Eugene, though but seventeen years of age, had joined Napoleon in the field as one of his aids, and had signalized himself by many acts of bravery.

In this arrangement we see an indication of the plans of boundless ambition which were already maturing in the mind of Bonaparte. The Italians hated their proud and domineering masters, the Austrians. They almost adored Napoleon as their deliverer. He had established the Cisalpine Republic, and conferred upon them a degree of liberty which for ages they had not enjoyed. Napoleon had but to unfurl his banner, and the Italians, in countless thousands, were ready to rally around it. The army in Italy regarded the Little Corporal with sentiments of veneration and affection, for which we may search history in vain for a parallel. Italy consequently became the base of Napoleon's operations. There he was strongly intrenched. In case of failure in any of his operations in Paris, he could retire behind the Alps, and bid defiance to his foes.

Josephine was exactly the partner he needed to protect these all-important interests during his absence. Her strong and active intelligence, her sincerity, her unrivaled powers of fascinating all who approached her, and her entire devotion to Napoleon, rendered her an ally of exceeding efficiency. Powerful as was the arm of Napoleon, he never could have risen to the greatness he attained without the aid of Josephine. She, at Milan, kept up the splendor of a royal court. The pleasure-loving Italians ever thronged her saloons. The most illustrious nobles were emulous to win her favor, that they might obtain eminence in the service of her renowned spouse. At the fêtes and entertainments she gave to the rejoicing Milanese she obtained access to almost every mind it was desirable to influence. No one could approach Josephine without becoming her friend, and a friend once gained was never lost. A weak woman, under these circumstances, which so severely tested the character, would have been often extremely embarrassed, and would have made many mistakes. It was remarkable in Josephine, that, notwithstanding the seclusion of her childhood and early youth, she ever appeared self-possessed, graceful, and at home in every situation in which she was placed. She moved through the dazzling scenes of her court at Milan, scenes of unaccustomed brilliance which had so suddenly burst upon her, with an air as entirely natural and unembarrassed as if her whole life had been passed in the saloons of monarchs. She conversed with the most distinguished generals of armies, with nobles of the highest rank, with statesmen and scholars of wide-spread renown, with a fluency, an appropriateness, and an inimitable tact which would seem to indicate that she had been cradled in the lap of princes, and nurtured in the society of courts. It seemed never to be necessary for her to study the rules of etiquette. She was never accustomed to look to others to ascertain what conduct was proper under any circumstances. Instinctive delicacy was her unerring teacher, and from her bearing others compiled their code of politeness. She became the queen of etiquette, not the subject.

Thus, while Napoleon, in Paris, was cautiously scrutinizing the state of public affairs, and endeavoring to gain a position there, Josephine, with the entire concentration of all her energies to his interests, was gaining for him in Milan vast accessions of power. She had no conception, indeed, of the greatness he was destined to attain. But she loved her husband. She was proud of his rising renown, and it was her sole ambition to increase, in every way in her power, the luster of his name. Aristocracy circled around her in delighted homage, while poverty, charmed by her sympathy and her beneficence, ever greeted her with acclamations. The exploits of Napoleon dazzled the world, and the unthinking world has attributed his greatness to his own unaided arm. But the gentleness of Josephine was one of the essential elements in the promotion of his greatness. In co-operation with her, he rose. As soon as he abandoned her, he fell.

Josephine soon rejoined her husband in Paris, where she very essentially aided, by her fascinating powers of persuasion, in disarming the hostility of those who were jealous of his rising fame, and in attaching to him such adherents as could promote his interests. In the saloons of Josephine, many of the most heroic youths of France were led to ally their fortunes with those of the young general, whose fame had so suddenly burst upon the world. She had the rare faculty of diffusing animation and cheerfulness wherever she appeared. "It is," she once beautifully remarked, "a necessity of my heart to love others, and to be loved by them in return." "There is only one occasion," she again said, "in which I would voluntarily use the words *I will*, namely, when I would say, '*I will* that all around me be happy.'"

Napoleon singularly displayed his knowledge of human nature in the course he pursued upon his return to Paris. He assumed none of the pride of a conqueror. He studiously avoided every thing like ostentatious display. Day after day his lieutenants arrived, bringing the standards taken from the Austrians. Pictures, and statues, and other works of art extorted from the conquered, were daily making their appearance, keeping the metropolis in a state of the most intense excitement. The Parisians were never weary of reading and re-reading those extraordinary proclamations of Napoleon, which, in such glowing language, described his almost miraculous victories. The enthusiasm of the people was thus raised to the highest pitch. The anxiety of the public to see this young and mysterious victor was intense beyond description. But he knew enough of the human heart to be conscious that, by avoiding the gratification of these wishes, he did but enhance their intensity. Modestly retiring to an unostentatious mansion in the Rue Chantereine, which, in compliment to him, had received the name of Rue de la Victoire, he secluded himself from the public gaze. He devoted his time most assiduously to study, and to conversation with learned men. He laid aside his military garb, and assumed the plain dress of a member of the Institute. When he walked the streets, he was seldom recognized by the people. Though his society was courted in the highest circles of Paris, his ambition was too lofty to be gratified with shining among the stars of fashion. Though he had as yet reached but the twenty-sixth year of his age, he had already gained the reputation of being the first of generals. He was emulous not only of appearing to be, but also of actually being, an accomplished scholar. "I well knew," said he, "that the lowest drummer in the army would respect me more for being a scholar as well as a soldier."

Napoleon might have enriched himself beyond all bounds in his Italian campaign had he been disposed to do so. Josephine, at times, remonstrated against his personal habits of economy, while he was conferring millions added to millions upon France. But the ambition of her husband, inordinate as it was, was as sublime an ambition as any one could feel in view of merely worldly interests. He wished to acquire the renown of benefiting mankind by the performance of the noblest exploits. His ultimate end was his own fame. But he knew that the durability of that fame could only be secured by the accomplishment of noble ends.

The effeminate figure of Napoleon in these early days had caused the soldiers to blend with their amazed admiration of his military genius a kind of fondness of affection for which no parallel can be found in ancient or modern story. The soldiers were ever rehearsing to one another, by their night-fires and in their long marches, anecdotes of his perfect fearlessness, his brilliant sayings, his imperious bearing, by which he overawed the haughtiness of aristocratic power, and his magnanimous acts toward the poor and the lowly.

One night, when the army in Italy was in great peril, worn out with the fatigue of sleeplessness and of battle, and surrounded by Austrians, Napoleon was taking the round of his posts in disguise, to ascertain the vigilance of his sentinels. He found one poor soldier, in perfect exhaustion, asleep at his post. Napoleon shouldered his musket, and stood sentry for him for half an hour. When the man awoke and recognized the countenance of his general, he sank back upon the ground in terror and despair. He knew that death was the doom for such a crime. "Here, comrade," said Napoleon, kindly, "here is your musket. You have fought hard and marched long, and your sleep is excusable. But a moment's inattention might at present ruin the army. I happened to be awake, and have guarded your post for you. You will be more careful another time."

At the "terrible passage of the bridge of Lodi," Napoleon stood at one of the guns, in the very hottest of the fire, directing it with his own hand. The soldiers, delighted at this very unusual exhibition of the readiness of their general to share all the toils and perils of the humblest private in the ranks, gave him the honorary and affectionate nickname of "The Little Corporal." By this appellation he was afterward universally known in the army. The enthusiasm of the soldiers invested him with supernatural endowments, and every one was ready at any moment to peril life for the Little Corporal.

The government at Paris, rapidly waning in popularity, notwithstanding their extreme jealousy of the wide-spreading influence of this victorious general, was compelled, by the spontaneous acclamations of the people, to give him a public triumph, when the famous treaty which Napoleon had effected in Italy was to be formally presented to the Directory. The magnificent court of the Luxembourg was embellished with the flags of the armies which he had conquered, and the youthful hero of Lodi, of Arcola, and of Rivoli made his first triumphant appearance in the streets of Paris. The enthusiasm of the vast concourse of excitable Parisians overleaped all bounds. The soldiers of the proud army of Italy sang at their encampments, in enthusiastic chorus, a song in which they declared that it was high time to eject the lawyers from the government, and make the Little Corporal the ruler of France. Barras, the friend of Josephine, who had selected Napoleon to quell the insurrection in Paris, and who had secured to him the command of the army of Italy, declared in a eulogistic speech on this occasion that "Nature had exhausted all her powers in the creation of a Bonaparte." This sentiment was received with the most deafening peals of applause.

But how like the phantasmagoria of magic has this change burst upon the bewildered Josephine. But a few months before, her husband, wan and wasted with imprisonment and woe, had been led from the subterranean dungeons of this very palace, with the execrations of the populace torturing his ear, to bleed upon the scaffold. She, also, was then herself a prisoner, without even a pillow for her weary head, awaiting the dawn of the morning which was to conduct her steps to a frightful death. Her children, Hortense and Eugene, had been rescued from homelessness, friendlessness, and beggary only by the hand of charity, and were dependent upon that charity for shelter and for daily bread. Now the weeds of widowhood have given place to the robes of the rejoicing bride, and that palace is gorgeously decorated in honor of the world-renowned companion upon whose arm she proudly leans. The acclamations resounding to his praise reverberate over mountain and valley, through every city and village of France. Princes, embassadors, and courtiers obsequiously crowd the saloons of Josephine. Eugene, an officer in the army, high in rank and honor, is lured along life's perilous pathway by the most brilliant prospects. Hortense in dazzling beauty, and surrounded by admirers, is intoxicated with the splendor, which, like Oriental enchantment, has burst upon her view.

Josephine, so beautifully called "the Star of Napoleon," was more than the harbinger of his rising. She gave additional luster to his brilliance, and was as the gentle zephyr, which sweeps away the mists and vapors, and presents a transparent sky through which the undimmed luminary may shine. Her persuasive influence was unweariedly and most successfully exerted in winning friends and in disarming adversaries. The admiration which was excited for the stern warrior in his solitary, silent, unapproachable grandeur, whose garments had been dyed in blood, whose fearful path had been signalized by conflagrations, and shrieks, and the wailings of the dying, was humanized and softened by the gentle loveliness of his companion, who was ever a ministering angel, breathing words of kindness, and diffusing around her the spirit of harmony and love. Napoleon ever freely acknowledged his indebtedness to Josephine for her aid in these morning hours of his greatness.

But unalloyed happiness is never allotted to mortals. Josephine's very loveliness of person and of character was to her the occasion of many hours of heaviness. No one could be insensible to the power of her attractions. The music of her voice, the sweetness of her smile, the grace of her manners, excited so much admiration, invested her with a popularity so universal and enthusiastic, that Napoleon was, at times, not a little disturbed by jealousy. Her appearance was ever the signal for crowds to gather around her. The most distinguished and the most gallant men in France vied with each other in doing her homage. Some of the relatives of Napoleon, envious of the influence she exerted over her illustrious spouse, and anxious, by undermining her power, to subserve their own interests, were untiring in their endeavors to foster all these jealousies. Josephine was exceedingly pained by the occasional indications of her husband's distrust. A word from his lips, a glance from his eye, often sent her to her chamber with weeping eyes and an aching heart. An interview with her husband, however, invariably removed his suspicions, and he gave her renewed assurances of his confidence and his love.

The plans of Napoleon in reference to his future operations were still in a state of great uncertainty. His restless spirit could not brook inactivity. He saw clearly that the time had not yet come in which he could, with the prospect of success, undertake to overthrow the Revolutionary government and grasp the reins of power himself. To use his own expressive language, "The pear was not yet ripe." To one of his intimate friends he remarked, "They do not long preserve at Paris the remembrance of any thing. If I remain any length of time unemployed, I am undone. The renown of one, in this great Babylon, speedily supplants that of another. If I am seen three times at the opera, I shall no longer be an object of curiosity. You need not talk of the desire of the citizens to see me. Crowds, at least as great, would go to see me led out to the scaffold. I am determined not to remain in Paris. There is nothing here to be done. Every thing here passes away. My glory is already declining. This little corner of Europe is too small to supply it. We must go to the East. All the great men of the world have there acquired their celebrity. We will go to Egypt."

Such was the grandeur of the dreams of a young man who had not yet passed his twenty-sixth year. And these were not the musings of a wild and visionary brain, but the deeply laid and cautiously guarded plans of a mind which had meditated profoundly upon all probable emergencies, and which had carefully weighed all the means which could be furnished for the accomplishment of an enterprise so arduous and so majestic.

7

Josephine at Malmaison

A.D. 1796-A.D. 1799

The Directory in Paris became daily more and more alarmed, in view of the vast and ever-increasing popularity of the conqueror of Italy. A plan had been formed for the invasion of England, and this was deemed a good opportunity for sending from France their dangerous rival. Napoleon was appointed commander-in-chief of the army of England. He visited the coast, and devoted ten days and nights, with his extraordinary rapidity of apprehension, in investigating the prospects of success. He returned to Paris, saying, "It is too doubtful a chance. I will not hazard on such a throw the fate of France." All his energies were then turned to his Egyptian expedition. He hoped to gain reputation and power in Egypt, pass through into India, raise an army of natives, headed by European officers and energized by an infusion of European soldiers, and thus drive the English out of India. It was a bold plan. The very grandeur of the enterprise roused the enthusiasm of France. The Directory, secretly rejoicing at the prospect of sending Napoleon so far away, and hoping that he would perish on the sands of Africa, without much reluctance agreed to his proposal.

Napoleon never loved the Revolution, and he most thoroughly detested the infamous and sanguinary despotism which had risen upon the ruins of the altar and the throne. He chanced to be in Paris when the drunken and ragged mob, like an inundation, broke into the Tuilleries, and heaped upon the humiliated Louis XVI. and Maria Antoinette the most infamous outrages. He saw the monarch standing at the window of his palace, with the dirty red cap of Jacobinism thrust upon that brow which had worn the crown of Charlemagne. At the sight, the blood boiled in the veins of the youthful Napoleon. He could not endure the spectacle. Turning upon his heel, he indignantly exclaimed, "The wretches! had they mown down four or five hundred with grape-shot, the rest would speedily have taken to flight."

He often expressed his dislike of the violent revolutionary course which the Directory were pursuing, and stated freely to his friends, "For my part, I declare, that if I had only the option between royalty and the system of these gentlemen, I would not hesitate for one moment to declare for a king." Just before Napoleon embarked for the East, Bourrienne asked him if he was really determined to risk his fate on the perilous expedition to Egypt. "Yes!" he replied. "If I should remain here, it would be necessary to overturn this miserable government, and make myself king. But we must not think of that yet. The nobles will not consent to it. I have sounded, but I find the time for that has not yet arrived. I must first dazzle these gentlemen by my exploits."

On the morning of the 19th of May, 1798, the fleet set sail from the harbor of Toulon. It was a morning of surpassing loveliness, and seldom, if ever, has the unclouded sun shone upon a more brilliant scene. The magnificent armament extended over a semicircle of not less than eighteen miles. The fleet consisted of thirteen ships of the line, fourteen frigates, and four hundred transports. They carried forty thousand picked soldiers, and officers of the highest celebrity. For the first time in the world, a corps of scientific gentlemen was attached to a military expedition. One hundred eminent artists and connoisseurs Napoleon had collected to gather the antiquarian treasures of Egypt, and to extend the boundaries of science by the observation of the phenomena of nature. They formed a part of the staff of the invading army.

Josephine accompanied her husband to Toulon, and remained with him until his embarkation. She was extremely anxious to go with him to Egypt, and with tears plead that he would allow her to share his hardships and his perils. Napoleon, however, deemed the hazards to which they would be exposed, and the fatigues and sufferings they must necessarily endure, as quite too formidable for Josephine to encounter. But in the anguish of their parting, which is described as most tender, she wrung from him a promise to allow her to follow as soon as affairs in the East should render it prudent for her to do so. It can hardly be possible, however, that Napoleon ever expected to see her in Egypt. He himself has thus described the objects he had in view in this vast enterprise:

"To:

1. Establish on the banks of the Nile a French colony, which could exist without slaves, and supply the place of Saint Domingo.

2. To open a market for the manufactures of France in Africa, Arabia, and Syria, and to obtain for the productions of his countrymen the productions of those countries.

3. To set out from Egypt, with an army of sixty thousand men, for the Indus, rouse the Mahrattas to a revolt, and excite against the English the population of those vast countries.

Sixty thousand men, half Europeans, half natives, transported on fifty thousand camels and ten thousand horses, carrying with them provisions for fifty days, water for six, with one hundred and fifty pieces of cannon and double ammunition, would arrive in four months in India. The ocean ceased to be an obstacle when vessels were constructed. The desert becomes passable the moment you have camels and dromedaries in abundance."

As the fleet got under way, Josephine stood upon a balcony, with tearful eyes, gazing upon the scene, so imposing, and yet so sorrowful to her. The Orient, a ship of enormous magnitude, contained her husband and her son. They were going into the midst of dangers from whence it was doubtful whether they would ever return. She fixed her eyes upon the ship as its lessening sails grew fainter and fainter in the distance, until the hardly discernible speck disappeared beneath the horizon, which the blue waves of the Mediterranean outlined. She retired to her room with those feelings of loneliness and desolation which the circumstances were so peculiarly calculated to inspire.

It was arranged that Josephine should take up her residence, until Napoleon should send for her, at Plombières, a celebrated watering-place, whose medicinal springs were supposed to be very efficacious in restoring maternity. She sent for Hortense, at that time fifteen years of age, and who was then in the boarding-school of the distinguished Madame Campan. Josephine wished for her daughter to be her companion during the weary hours of her absence from her husband. She was expecting that, as soon as a landing should be effected in Egypt, a frigate would be dispatched to convey her to the banks of the Nile. She found solace during the lingering weeks of expectation in devoting herself to the instruction of her daughter. Her comprehensive and excellent views on the subject of education are developed in a letter which she at this time wrote to Madame Campan, to accompany a niece who was to return to her school:

"My dear Madame Campan,—

With my niece, whom I return to your charge, receive also my thanks and my reproof. The former are due for the great care and brilliant education which you have bestowed upon the child; the latter, for the faults which your sagacity must have discovered, but which your indulgence has tolerated. The girl is gentle, but shy; well informed, but haughty; talented, but thoughtless. She does not please, and takes no pains to render herself agreeable. She conceives that the reputation of her uncle and the bravery of her father are every thing. Teach her, and that by the most effectual means, how absolutely unavailing are those qualities which are not personal. We live in an age where each is the author of his own fortunes; and if those who serve the state in the first ranks ought to have some advantages and enjoy some privileges, they should, on that account, strive only to render themselves more beloved and more useful. It is solely by acting thus that they can have some chance of excusing their good fortune in the eyes of envy. Of these things, my dear Madame Campan, you must not allow my niece to remain ignorant; and such are the instructions which, in my name, you should repeat to her constantly. It is my pleasure that she treat as equals every one of her companions, most of whom are better or as good as herself, their only inferiority consisting in not having relations so able or so fortunate."

Notwithstanding Napoleon's strong disinclination to have Josephine join him in Egypt, and though in every letter he strongly urged her to relinquish the plan, she was so importunate in her solicitations that he sent the Pomona frigate to convey her across the Mediterranean. She was prevented from embarking by an accident, which she must have deemed a very serious calamity, but which probably saved her from years of captivity. She was one morning sitting in her saloon, busy with her needle, and conversing with several ladies who were her companions and intimate friends, when a lady who was standing in the balcony called the attention of the party to a very beautiful dog which was passing in the street. All the ladies rushed upon the balcony, when, with a fearful crash, it broke down, and precipitated them upon the pavement. Though no lives were lost, several of the party were dreadfully injured. Josephine was so severely bruised as to be utterly helpless, and for some time she was fed like an infant. It was several months before she was sufficiently recovered to be able to leave her house. This grievous disappointment, however, probably saved her from another, which would have been far more severely felt. The frigate in which she was to have embarked, had it not been for this accident, was captured by one of the English cruisers and taken to London.

Napoleon went to Egypt because he thought it the shortest route to the vacant throne of the Bourbons. He despised the rulers who were degrading France, and placing a stigma upon popular liberty by their ignorance and their violence, and he resolved upon their overthrow. Consequently, while guiding the movements of his army upon the banks of the Nile, his attention was continually directed to Paris. He wrote to Josephine that he intended ere long to return, and directed her to purchase a pleasant country seat somewhere in the vicinity of Paris.

About ten miles from the metropolis and five miles from Versailles there was a beautiful chateau, most charmingly situated, called Malmaison. This estate Josephine purchased, greatly enlarging the grounds, at an expense of about one hundred thousand dollars. This lovely retreat possessed unfailing rural attraction for a mind formed, like that of Josephine, for the rich appreciation of all that is lovely in the aspects of nature. Napoleon was delighted with the purchase, and expended subsequently incredible sums in repairs and enlargements, and in embellishments of statues, paintings, and furniture. This was ever the favorite residence of Napoleon and Josephine.

As the leaves of autumn began to fall, Josephine, who had been slowly recovering from the effects of the accident, left Plombières and took up her residence at Malmaison. Napoleon was absent in Egypt about eighteen months. During the winter and the ensuing summer, Josephine remained with Hortense, and several other ladies, who composed her most agreeable household, in this beautiful retreat. The celebrity of Napoleon surrounded them with friends, and that elegant mansion was the resort of the most illustrious in rank and intellect. Napoleon, who had ever a spice of jealousy in his nature, had every thing reported to him which occurred at Malmaison. He was informed respecting all the guests who visited the chateau, and of the conversation which passed in every interview.

Hortense was a lively girl of fifteen, and the time hung rather heavily upon her hands. She amused herself in playing all manner of pranks upon a very singular valet de chambre, by the name of Carrat, whom her mother had brought from Italy. This man was very timid and eccentric, but, with most enthusiastic devotion, attached to the service of Josephine.

One evening Carrat received orders to attend Madame Bonaparte and several ladies who were with her in their twilight walk through the magnificent park belonging to the estate. Carrat, ever delighted with an opportunity to display his attachment to his kind mistress, obeyed with great alacrity. No ladies in peril could desire a more valiant knight-errant than the vaunting little Italian assumed to be. They had not advanced far into the somber shadows of the grove when they saw, solemnly emerging from the obscurity, a tall specter in its winding-sheet. The fearful apparition approached the party, when the valet, terrified beyond all power of self-control, and uttering the most fearful shrieks, abandoned the ladies to the tender mercies of the ghost, and fled. The phantom, with its white drapery fluttering in the wind, pursued him. Soon the steps of the affrighted valet began to falter, and he dropped upon the ground, insensible, in a fit. Hortense, who had been perfectly convulsed with laughter in view of the triumphant success of her experiment, was now correspondingly alarmed. The ghost was a fellow-servant of Carrat, who had been dressed out under the superintendence of the mischievous Hortense.

As the poor man recovered without any serious injury and without the slightest diminution of his excessive vanity, the fun-loving Hortense could not repress her propensity still to make him the butt of her practical jokes. It was a defect in her character that she could find pleasure in this mischievous kind of torment. It is not improbable that this trait of character, which appears so excusable in a mirthful girl of fifteen, was the cause of that incessant train of sorrows which subsequently embittered her whole life. Carrat was perfectly devoted to Josephine; Hortense was his torment.

The unlucky valet occupied a sleeping-room separated from another only by a thin deal partition. A hole was made through this, and a pail of water so suspended in equilibrium over the pillow of the victim, that by drawing a cord the whole contents would be emptied upon his head. The supports of the bedstead had also been removed, so that the whole fabric would fall as soon as any weight was placed upon it. Carrat, among his other eccentricities, was ever in the habit of going to bed without a light. Matters being thus prepared, Hortense, who had employed an attendant to aid her in her plans, stood in an adjoining room to enjoy the catastrophe.

The poor man entered his room, and threw himself upon his pallet. Down it came with a crash, and his shriek of fright was for a moment drowned in the inundation of water. Hortense, knowing the almost delirious fear which the puerile valet had of reptiles, cried, "Poor man! poor man! what will he do. The water was full of toads." Carrat, in utter darkness, drenched with cold water, and overwhelmed in the ruins of his bed and bedding, shrieked, "Murder! help! fire! drowning!" while Hortense and her accomplices enjoyed his ludicrous terror. She afterward made him a handsome present as a compensation. Hortense was not a malicious girl, but, like many others who are mirthful and thoughtless, she found a strange pleasure in teasing. Josephine's only happiness was in making others happy. "It is a necessity of my heart," she said, "to love those around me, and to be loved by them in return." How much more noble such a spirit!

Though Josephine was not fully informed respecting the ultimate designs of Napoleon, and though Napoleon at this time probably had no very definite plans respecting his future actions, his interests manifestly required that she should exert all her powers to strengthen the ties of those who were already his friends, and to gain others to his rising name. Josephine acquired great influence over many members of the Directory, and this influence she was continually exerting for the relief of those who were in distress. Many of the proscribed emigrants were indebted to her for liberty and the restoration of their forfeited estates. The following letter from Josephine to an emigrant, whose fortune, and perhaps life, she had saved, exhibits her intellectual elevation as well as the amiability of her heart.

"Sir,—

Your petition, which reached Malmaison on the 12th, was presented the same evening, and by myself, to Citizen Barras. I have the pleasure to announce to you that the decision is favorable, and that now, erased from the fatal list, you are restored to all the rights of a French citizen. But in transmitting a communication not less agreeable to me than to yourself, permit me to enhance its value by repeating to you the exact words with which it was accompanied by the Director. 'I have usually little to deny you, madame,' said he, presenting me with a sealed inclosure containing the act of restoration, 'and certainly, when humanity is concerned, I can have far less objection. But pity for misfortune does not exclude justice, and justice is inseparable from the love of truth. As unfortunate, M. de Sansal merits commiseration. As an emigrant, he has right to none. I will say more; had I been disposed to be severe, there existed a cause for stern reprisals on the part of a government to whose kindness he replies by insults. Although I despise those of such a man, I appreciate them. They prove an ungrateful heart and a narrow mind. Let him be careful about expressing his hatred. All my colleagues are not equally indulgent.'

"Blame only yourself, sir, for the small share of amenity in these counsels. They are harsh, perhaps, but useful; and you will do well to render them effective. Regard, also, the faithfulness with which I transcribe them as a proof of the deep interest I take in your welfare, and of my anxiety that the interference of your friends may be justified by your future conduct."

For some time a very constant correspondence was kept up between Napoleon and Josephine, but after the destruction of the French fleet by Lord Nelson in the Bay of Aboukir, and when the Mediterranean had become completely blocked up by English cruisers, almost every letter was intercepted.

For political purposes, there were many who wished to destroy the influence which Josephine had acquired over the mind of her illustrious husband. In the accomplishment of this plan, they endeavored, in every way in their power, to excite the jealousy of Napoleon. The very efforts which Josephine was making to attract the most influential men in Paris to her saloon were represented to him as indications of levity of character, and of a spirit of unpardonable coquetry. The enemies of Josephine had their influential agents in the camp of Napoleon, and with malice, never weary, they whispered these suspicions into his ear. The jealousy of his impassioned nature was strongly aroused. In his indignation, he wrote to Josephine in terms of great severity, accusing her of "playing the coquette with all the world." She was very deeply wounded by these unjust suspicions, and wrote to him a letter in reply, which, for tenderness and delicacy of sentiment, and the expression of conscious innocence, is hardly surpassed by any thing which has ever been written. Her letter was intercepted, and Napoleon never saw it. For many months nearly all communication with the army of Egypt was cut off by the vigilance of the English. There were flying reports ever reaching the ear of Josephine of disaster to the army, and even of the death of Napoleon. Josephine was at times in great distress. She knew not the fate of her husband or her son. She knew that, by the grossest deception, her husband's confidence in her had been greatly impaired, and she feared that, should he return, she might never be able to regain his affections. Still, she devoted herself with unwearied diligence in watching over all his interests, and though her heart was often oppressed with anguish, she did every thing in her power to retain the aspect of cheerfulness and of sanguine hope. One of her favorite amusements—the favorite amusement of almost every refined mind—was found in the cultivation of flowers. She passed a portion of every pleasant day with Hortense among the flower-beds, with the hoe, and the watering-pot, and the pruning-knife. Hortense, though she loved the society of her mother, was not fond of these employments, and in subsequent life she never turned to them for a solace. With Josephine, however, this taste remained unchanged through life. She was also very fond of leaving the aristocratic walks of Malmaison, and sauntering through the lanes and the rural roads, where she could enter the cottages of the peasants, and listen to their simple tales of joy and grief. To many of these dwellings her visit was as the mission of an angel. Her purse was never closed against the wants of penury. But that which rendered her still more a ministering spirit to the poor was that her heart was ever open, with its full flood of sympathy, to share the grief of their bereavements, and to rejoice in their joy. When she sat upon the throne of France, and even long after she sank into the repose of the grave, the region around Malmaison was full of recitals of her benevolence. Aristocratic pride at times affected to look down with contempt upon the elevated enjoyments of a noble heart.

Thus occupied in pleading with those in power for those of illustrious birth who had, by emigration, forfeited both property and life; in visiting the sick and the sorrowing in the humble cottages around her; in presiding with queenly dignity over the brilliant soirées in her own saloons, where talent and rank were ever assembled, and in diffusing the sunlight of her own cheerful heart throughout the whole household at Malmaison, Josephine, through weary months, awaited tidings from her absent husband.

8

Josephine the Wife of the First Consul

A.D. 1799-A.D. 1800

The winter of 1799 opened upon France in the deepest gloom. The French were weary of the horrors of the Revolution. All business was at a stand. The poor had neither employment nor bread. Starvation reigned in the capital. The Austrians had again entered Italy, and beaten the French at almost every point. No tidings were received from Bonaparte and the army in Egypt. Rumors of the death of Napoleon and of a disastrous state of the enterprise filled the city. The government at Paris, composed of men who had emerged from obscurity in the storms of revolution, was imbecile and tyrannical in the extreme. The nation was weary beyond endurance of the strife of contending factions, and ardently desired some strong arm to be extended for the restoration of order, and for the establishment of an efficient and reputable government. "The pear was ripe."

On the evening of the 9th of November, a large and very brilliant party was assembled in Paris at the house of M. Gohier, president of the Directory. The company included all the most distinguished persons then resident in the metropolis. Josephine, being in Paris at that time, was one of the guests. About midnight, the gentlemen and ladies were gathering around a supper table very sumptuously spread, when they were startled by a telegraphic announcement, communicated to their host, that Bonaparte had landed that morning at Frejus, a small town upon the Mediterranean shore. The announcement created the most profound sensation. All knew that Napoleon had not returned at that critical moment without an object. Many were pale with apprehension, conscious that his popularity with the army would enable him to wrest from them their ill-gotten power. Others were elated with hope. Yet universal embarrassment prevailed. None dared to express their thoughts. No efforts could revive the conviviality of the evening, and the party soon dispersed.

Josephine, with the deepest emotion, hastened home, immediately summoned her carriage, and, taking with her Hortense and Louis Bonaparte, set out, without allowing an hour for repose, to meet her husband. She was very anxious to have an interview with him before her enemies should have an opportunity to fill his mind with new accusations against her. The most direct route from Paris to Frejus passes through the city of Lyons. There is another and more retired route, not frequently traveled, but which Napoleon, for some unknown reason, took. It was a long journey of weary, weary leagues, over hills and plains. Josephine alighted not for refreshment or slumber, but with fresh relays of horses, night and day, pressed on to meet her spouse. When she arrived at Lyons, to her utter consternation, she heard that Napoleon had taken the other route, and, some forty-eight hours before, had passed her on the way to Paris. No words can describe the anguish which these tidings caused her. Her husband would arrive in Paris and find her absent. He would immediately be surrounded by those who would try to feed his jealousy. Two or three days must elapse ere she could possibly retrace her steps. Napoleon arrived in Paris the 10th of November. It was not until nearly midnight of the 13th that Josephine returned. Worn out with the fatigues of traveling, of anxiety, and of watching, she drove with a heavy heart to their house in the Rue Chantereine.

The enemies whom Josephine had most to fear were the brothers and the sisters-in-law of Napoleon. They were entirely dependent upon their illustrious brother for their own advancement in life, and were exceedingly jealous of the influence which Josephine had exerted over his mind. They feared that she would gain an exclusive empire where they wished also to reign. Taking advantage of Josephine's absence, they had succeeded in rousing Napoleon's indignation to the highest pitch. They accused her of levity, of extravagance, of forgetfulness of him, and of ever playing the coquette with all the debauchees of Paris. Napoleon, stimulated by that pride which led the Roman emperor to say, "Cæsar's wife must not be suspected," threatened loudly "divorce—open and public divorce." Said one maliciously to him, "She will appear before you with all her fascinations, explain matters; you will forgive all, and tranquillity will be restored." "Never! never!" exclaimed the irritated general, striding to and fro through the room. "I forgive! never! You know me. Were I not sure of my resolution, I would pluck out this heart and cast it into the fire."

Such was the mood of mind in which Napoleon was prepared to receive Josephine, after an absence of eighteen months. Josephine and Hortense alighted in the court-yard, and were immediately enfolded in the embraces of Eugene, who was anxiously awaiting their arrival. With trembling steps and a throbbing heart, Josephine, accompanied by her son and daughter, ascended the stairs to a small circular family room where they expected to find Napoleon. He was there with his brother Joseph. As his wife and her children entered the room, Napoleon glanced sternly at them, and instantly said to Josephine, in a severe and commanding tone, almost before she had crossed the threshold,

"Madame! it is my wish that you retire immediately to Malmaison."

Josephine came near falling lifeless upon the floor. She was caught in the arms of Eugene, who, in the most profound grief, had kept near the side of his revered and beloved mother. He supported her fainting steps, as, sobbing with anguish, she silently retired to her apartment. Napoleon, greatly agitated, traversed the room with hasty strides. The sight of Josephine had rekindled all his love, and he was struggling with desperate efforts to cherish his sense of wrong, and to fortify himself against any return of clemency.

The Interview.

In a few moments, Josephine and Hortense, with Eugene, were heard descending the stairs to leave the house. It was midnight. For a week Josephine had lived in her carriage almost without food or sleep. Nothing but intensity of excitement had prevented her from sinking down in utter weariness and exhaustion. It was a drive of thirty miles to Malmaison. Napoleon was not prepared for such prompt obedience. Even his stern heart could not resist its instinctive pleadings for his wife and her daughter. He hastened from his room, and, though his pride would not allow him directly to urge *Josephine* to remain, he insisted upon Eugene's returning, and urged it in such a way that he came back, leading with him his mother and his sister. Napoleon, however, addressed not a word to either of them. Josephine threw herself upon a couch in her apartment, and Napoleon, in gloomy silence, entered his cabinet. Two days of wretchedness passed away, during which no intercourse took place between the estranged parties. But the anger of the husband was gradually subsiding. Love for Josephine was slowly gaining strength in his heart. On the third day, his pride and passion were sufficiently subdued to allow him to enter the apartment where Josephine and Hortense had kept themselves secluded, awaiting his pleasure. Josephine was seated at a toilet table, with her face buried in her hands, and absorbed in the profoundest grief. On the table were exposed the letters which she had received from Napoleon during his absence, and which she had evidently been reading. Hortense was standing silently and pensively in an alcove by the window, half concealed by the curtain. Napoleon advanced with an irresolute step, hesitated for a moment, and then said, "Josephine!" She started up at the sound of that well-known voice, and, her beautiful countenance all suffused with tears, mournfully exclaimed, "*Mon ami*," in that peculiar tone, so pathetic, so musical, which ever thrilled upon the heart of Napoleon. "My friend" was the term of endearment with which she invariably addressed her husband. Napoleon was vanquished. He extended his hand to his deeply-wronged wife. She threw herself into his arms, pillowed her aching head upon his bosom, and in the fullness of blended joy and anguish wept convulsively. An explanation of several hours ensued. Every shade of suspicion was obliterated from his mind. He received Josephine again to his entire confidence, and this confidence was never again interrupted.

When Napoleon landed at Frejus, he was received with the most enthusiastic demonstration of delight. There was a universal impression that the hero of Italy, the conqueror of Egypt, had returned thus unexpectedly to France for the accomplishment of some magnificent enterprise; yet no one knew what to anticipate. The moment the frigate dropped anchor in the bay, and it was announced that Napoleon was on board, thousands surrounded the vessel in boats, and the air was filled with enthusiastic acclamations. His journey to Paris was one continued scene of triumph. Crowds gathered around him at every stopping-place, intoxicated with joy. The bells rang their merriest peals; the booming of cannon echoed along the hill sides, and brilliant bonfires by night blazed upon every eminence. Upon his arrival in Paris, the soldiers, recognizing their leader in so many brilliant victories, greeted him with indescribable enthusiasm, and cries of "Vive Bonaparte!" resounded through the metropolis. His saloon, ever thronged with generals and statesmen, and all who were most illustrious in intellect and rank, resembled the court of a monarch. Even the most prominent men in the Directory, disgusted with the progress of measures which they could not control, urged him to grasp the reins of power, assuring him that there was no hope for France but in his strong arm. In less than four weeks from his arrival in Paris, the execrated government was overturned. Napoleon, Siêyes, and Ducos were appointed consuls, and twenty-five members were appointed from each of the councils to unite with the consuls in forming a new Constitution. One unanimous voice of approval rose from all parts of France in view of this change. No political movement could take place more strongly confirmed by the popular will. Napoleon hastened from the scenes of peril and agitation through which he had passed in the accomplishment of this change, that he might be the first to announce to Josephine the political victory he had achieved.

During the perilous day, when, in the midst of outcries, daggers, and drawn swords, he had been contending with the Council of the Five Hundred, he could find not even one moment to dispatch a note from St. Cloud to his wife. The previous day he had kept her constantly informed of the progress of events. Josephine remained throughout the whole of the 19th of November, from morning until evening, without sight or tidings of her husband. She knew that, in the fierce strife of parties in France, there was no safety for life; and when the darkness of night settled down around her, and still no word from her Napoleon, her anxiety amounted almost to distraction. The rumbling of every carriage upon the pavement—every noise in the streets aroused her hopes or her fears. Worn out with anxiety, at midnight she threw herself upon her bed, but not to sleep. Several weary hours of suspense lingered slowly along, when, at four o'clock in the morning, she heard the well-known footsteps of her husband upon the stairs.

She sprang to meet him. He fondly clasped her in his arms, and assured her that he had not spoken to a single individual since he had taken the oaths of office, that the voice of his Josephine might be the first to congratulate him upon his virtual accession to the empire of France. An animated conversation ensued, and then Napoleon, throwing himself upon his couch for a few moments' repose, gayly said, "Good night, my Josephine! to-morrow we sleep in the Luxembourg."

The next day the three consuls met in Paris. His colleagues, however, immediately perceived that the towering ambition of Napoleon would brook no rival. He showed them the absurdity of their plans, and compelled them to assent to the superior wisdom of his own. The untiring vigor of his mind, the boldness and energy of his thoughts, and his intuitive and almost miraculous familiarity with every branch of political science, overawed his associates, and the whole power passed, with hardly the slightest resistance, into his own hands. Immediately after their first interview, the Abbé Siêyes, who combined great weakness with extensive knowledge, remarked to Talleyrand and others, "Gentlemen, I perceive that we have got a master. Bonaparte can do and will do every thing himself. But," he continued, after a pause, "it is better to submit than to protract dissensions forever."

In this most astonishing revolution, thus suddenly accomplished, and without the shedding of a drop of blood, Napoleon was much indebted to the influence which his wife had exerted in his behalf during his absence in Egypt. The dinners she had given, the guests she had entertained in her saloons evening after evening, consisting of the most distinguished scholars, and statesmen, and generals in the metropolis, had contributed greatly to the popularity of her husband, and had surrounded him with devoted friends. Napoleon ever acknowledged his obligations to Josephine for the essential service she had thus rendered him.

The next morning Napoleon and Josephine removed from their elegant yet comparatively plebeian residence in the Rue Chantereine to the palace of the Luxembourg. This, however, was but the stepping-stone to the Tuilleries, the world-renowned abode of the monarchs of France. They remained for two months at the Luxembourg. The energies of Napoleon were employed every moment in promoting changes in the internal affairs of France, which even his bitterest enemies admit were marked with the most eminent wisdom and benevolence. During the two months of their residence at the Luxembourg, no domestic event of importance occurred, except the marriage of Murat with Caroline, the sister of Napoleon. Caroline was exceedingly beautiful. Murat was one of the favorite aids of Bonaparte. Their nuptials were celebrated with great splendor, and the gay Parisians began again to be amused with something like the glitter of royalty.

Each day Napoleon became more popular and his power more firmly established. Soon all France was prepared to see the first consul take up his residence in the ancient apartments of the kings of France. The Tuilleries had been sacked again and again by the mob. The gorgeous furniture, the rich paintings, and all the voluptuous elegance which the wealth of Louis XIV. could create, had been thrown into the court-yard and consumed by the infuriated populace. Royalty itself had been pursued and insulted in its most sacred retreats.

By slow and cautious advances, Napoleon refurnished these magnificent saloons. The emblems of Jacobin misrule were silently effaced. Statues of Brutus and Washington, of Demosthenes, and of others renowned for illustrious deeds, were placed in the vacant niches, and the Tuilleries again appeared resplendent as in the days of pristine pride and power.

On the morning of the 19th of February, 1800, all Paris was in commotion to witness the transfer of the embryo court of the first consul and his colleagues from the Luxembourg to the Tuilleries. Already the colleagues of Napoleon had become so entirely eclipsed by the superior brilliance of their imperious associate that their names were almost forgotten. The royal apartments were prepared for Napoleon, while those in the Pavilion of Flora were assigned to the two other consuls. The three consuls entered a magnificent carriage, drawn by six white horses.

A gorgeous train of officers, with six thousand picked troops in the richest uniform, surrounded the cortège. Many of the long-abolished usages of royalty were renewed upon that day. Twenty thousand soldiers, in most imposing military array, were drawn up before the palace. The moment the carriage appeared, the very heavens seemed rent with their cries, "Vive le premier consul!" The two associate consuls were ciphers. They sat at his side as pages to embellish his triumph. This day placed Napoleon in reality upon the throne of France, and Josephine that evening moved, a queen, in the apartments hallowed by the beauty and the sufferings of Maria Antoinette.

The suite of rooms appropriated to the wife of the first consul consisted of two magnificent saloons, with private apartments adjoining. No French monarch ever sauntered through a more dazzling scene than that which graced the drawing-rooms of Josephine on this occasion. Embassadors from nearly all the courts of Europe were present. The army contributed its utmost display of rank and military pomp to embellish the triumph of its most successful general. And the metropolis contributed all that it still retained of brilliance in ancestral renown or in intellectual achievement.

When Josephine entered the gorgeously-illuminated apartments of the palace, leaning upon the arm of Talleyrand, and dressed in the elegance of the most perfect simplicity, a murmur of admiration arose from the whole assembly. She was attired in a robe of white muslin. Her hair fell in graceful ringlets upon her neck and shoulders. A necklace of pearls of great value completed her costume. The queenly elegance of her figure, the inimitable grace of her movements, the peculiar conversational tact she possessed, and the melody of a voice which, once heard, never was forgotten, gave to Josephine, on this eventful evening, a social triumph corresponding with that which Napoleon had received during the day. She entered the rooms to welcome her guests before her husband. As she made the tour of the apartments, supported by the minister, whose commanding figure towered above all the rest, she was first introduced to the foreign embassadors, and then to others of distinguished name and note. "Napoleon wins battles, but Josephine wins hearts." This was the all-appropriate theater for the triumph of Josephine. Here she was entirely at home. Instinct taught her every thing that was graceful and pleasing. Etiquette, that stern tyrant so necessary for the control of common minds, was compelled to bow in subjection to Josephine, for her actions became a higher law. In the exuberance of benevolent joy, she floated through this brilliant scene, wherever she appeared exciting admiration, though she sought only to diffuse enjoyment.

Josephine was now about thirty-three years of age, and while in personal charms she retained all the fascination of more youthful years, her mind, elevated and ennobled by reverses and sufferings most magnanimously borne, and cultivated by the daily exercise of its rich endowments, enabled her to pass from the circles of fashion to the circles of science, from those who thought only of the accomplishments of the person to those who dwelt in the loftiest regions of the intellect, and to be equally admired by both.

Her figure appears to have been molded into the absolute perfection of the female frame, The Interview.neither too large for the utmost delicacy of feminine beauty, nor too small for queenly dignity. The exquisite symmetry of her form and the elasticity of her step gave an etherial aspect to her movements. Her features, of Grecian outline, were finely modeled, and through them all the varying emotions of the soul were unceasingly beaming. No one probably ever possessed in a higher degree this resistless charm of feminine loveliness. Her eyes were of a deep blue, and possessed a winning tenderness of expression when reposing upon those she loved which could not be resisted. Napoleon, even when most agitated by the conflicts of his stormy life, was speedily subdued by the tranquilizing power of her looks of love. But the tone and modulations of her voice in conversation constituted the most remarkable attraction of this most attractive woman. No one could listen to her sparkling, flowing, musical words without feeling the fascination of their strange melody. "The first applauses of the French people," says Napoleon, "fell upon my ear sweet as the voice of Josephine."

The rural charms of Malmaison, however, exerted a more powerful sway over both the first consul and his companion than the more splendid attractions of the Tuilleries. The Revolutionary government had abolished the Sabbath, and appointed every tenth day for rest and recreation. Napoleon and Josephine habitually spent this day at Malmaison. There, in the retirement of green fields and luxuriant groves, surrounded by those scenes of nature which had peculiar charms for them both, they found that quiet happiness which is in vain sought amid the turmoil of the camp or the splendor of the court. Josephine, in particular, here found her most serene and joyous hours. She regretted the high ambition of her husband, while, at the same time, she felt a wife's pride and gratification in view of the honors which were so profusely heaped upon him. It delighted her to see him here lay aside the cares of state, and enjoy with her the unostentatious pleasures of the flower-garden and the farm-yard. And when the hour came for them to return from their rural villa to their city palace, Napoleon often said, with a sigh, "Now it is necessary for us to go and put on again the yoke of misery."

The dangers of greatness soon began to hover around the path of the first consul. Josephine was continually alarmed with rumors of conspiracies and plots of assassination. The utter indifference of Napoleon to all such perils, and his entire disregard of all precautionary measures, only increased the anxiety of his wife. The road leading from Paris to Malmaison wound through a wild district, then but thinly inhabited, and which presented many facilities for deeds of violence. Whenever Napoleon was about to traverse this road, Josephine sent the servants of their private establishment to scrutinize all its lurking-places where any foes might be concealed. Napoleon, though gratified by this kind care, often amused and good-naturedly teased Josephine with most ludicrous accounts of the perils and hair-breadth escapes which he had encountered. She also had large and powerful dogs trained to guard the grounds of Malmaison from any intrusion by night.

On the evening of the day when Napoleon made his entry into the Tuilleries, he remarked to Bourrienne, "It is not enough to be in the Tuilleries, we must take measures to remain there. Who has not inhabited this palace? It has been the abode of robbers—of the Convention. There is your brother's house, from which, eight years ago, we saw the good Louis XVI. besieged in the Tuilleries and carried off into captivity. But you need not fear a repetition of the scene. *Let them attempt it with me if they dare.*" To all the cautions of his anxious wife respecting assassination, he ever quietly replied, "My dear Josephine, they dare not do it."

9

Developments of Character

A.D. 1800-A.D. 1801

During Napoleon's absence in Egypt the Austrians had again invaded Italy. The French troops had been beaten in many battles, and driven from vast extents of territory, over which Napoleon had caused the flag of the Republic to float in triumph. The first consul having, with almost superhuman energy, arranged the internal affairs of his government, now turned his thoughts toward the defeated armies of France, which had been driven back into the fastnesses of the Alps. "I must go," said he, "my dear Josephine. But I will not forget you, and I will not be absent long." He bade adieu to his wife at the Tuilleries on the 7th of May, 1800. At midnight of the 2d of July he returned, having been absent less than two months. In that brief period he drove the Austrians from all their strongholds, regained Italy, and by a campaign more brilliant than any other which history has ever recorded, added immeasurably to his own moral power. These astonishing victories excited the Parisians to a delirium of joy. Night after night the streets were illuminated, and whenever Napoleon appeared, crowds thronged him, filling the air with their acclamations. These triumphs, however, instead of satisfying Napoleon, did but add fuel to his all-absorbing ambition. "A few more great events," said he, "like those of this campaign, and I may really descend to posterity. But still it is little enough. I have conquered, it is true, in less than two years, Cairo, Paris, Milan. But, were I to die to-morrow, half a page of general history would, after ten centuries, be all that would be devoted to my exploits."

During his absence Josephine passed her time at Malmaison. And it surely is indicative not only of the depth of Napoleon's love for Josephine, but also of his appreciation of those delicate attentions which could touch the heart of a loving wife, that in this busiest of campaigns, in which, by day and by night, he was upon the horse's back, with hardly one moment allowed for refreshment or repose, rarely did a single day pass in which he did not transmit some token of affection to Malmaison. Josephine daily watched, with the most intense interest the arrival of the courier with the brief and almost illegible note from her husband. Sometimes the blurred and blotted lines were hastily written upon horseback, with the pommel of his saddle for his writing-desk. Sometimes they were written, at his dictation, by his secretary, upon a drum-head, on the field of carnage, when the mangled bodies of the dying and the dead were strewed all around him, and the thunders of the retreating battle were still echoing over the plains. These delicate attentions to his wife exhibit a noble trait in the character of Napoleon. And she must have been indeed a noble woman who could have inspired such a mind with esteem and tenderness so profound.

Josephine employed much of her time in superintending those improvements which she thought would please her husband on his return; creating for him pleasant little surprises, as she should guide his steps to the picturesque walk newly opened, to the rustic bridge spanning the stream, to the rural pavilion, where, in the evening twilight, they could commune. She often rode on horseback with Hortense, who was peculiarly fond of all those pleasures which had the concomitants of graceful display.

After Napoleon's triumphant return from Italy, the visits to Malmaison were more frequent than ever before. Napoleon and Josephine often spent several days there; and in after years they frequently spoke of these hours as the pleasantest they had passed in life. The agreeable retirement of Malmaison was, however, changed into enjoyment more public and social by the crowds of visitors with which its saloons and parks were filled. Josephine received her guests with republican simplicity, united with the utmost elegance. Her reception-room was continually thronged with the most distinguished officers of the government, renowned generals, and all the men most illustrious for birth and talent the metropolis contained.

The circle assembled here was, indeed, a happy one. A peculiar bond of union existed throughout the whole household, for Napoleon, as well as Josephine, secured the most devoted attachment of all the servants. One of their favorite amusements was family theatricals. Eugene and Hortense took an active part in these performances, in which both had talents to excel.

But the favorite and most characteristic amusement at Malmaison was the game of "Prisoners," a common game among the school-boys of France, though comparatively little known in this country. The company is divided into two parties. Those who are appointed leaders choose each their respective sides. Bounds are assigned to each party, and a particular point as a fortress. If any one is caught away from the fortress by one who left his own station after the captive left the hostile fort, he is a prisoner, and must remain at the appointed prison until rescued. For instance, Hortense leaves her fortress, and cautiously invades the territory of the enemy. Josephine darts after her, and eagerly pursues her over the greensward. Eugene, who remains at his fortress until after Josephine left hers, bounds after his mother. It is now her turn to flee. But others of her party, who have remained under the protection of their fortress, rush to her rescue. Eugene, however, succeeds in touching his mother before they reach him, and leads her off in triumph a prisoner. A tree, perhaps, at a little distance, is her prison. Here she must remain until rescued by a touch from one of her own party. But if the one who is rushing to her rescue is touched by one of the other party who left his fortress an instant later, another captive is taken to stand by her side.

In this mimicry of war Napoleon always delighted to engage. After dinner, upon the lawn at Malmaison, the most distinguished gentlemen and ladies, not of France only, but of all Europe, were often actively and most mirthfully engaged in this sport. Kings, and queens, and princes of the blood royal were often seen upon the lawn at Malmaison pursuing and pursued. Napoleon and Josephine, and most of the friends who surrounded them, were in the vigor of athletic youth, and, in entire abandonment to the frolic of the hour, the air resounded with their shouts. It was observed that Napoleon was ever anxious to choose Josephine as the first on his side, and he seemed nervously excited, if she was taken prisoner, until she was rescued. He was a poor runner, and often fell, rolling over headlong upon the grass, while he and all his associates were convulsed with laughter. When there was no special engagement demanding attention, this sport often continued for hours. Napoleon was often taken captive. But when Josephine was imprisoned, he was incessantly clapping his hands, and shouting, "A rescue! a rescue!" till she was released. A gloomy misanthrope, wrapped in self, could not have enjoyed these scenes of innocent hilarity.

But the life of Josephine was not devoted to amusement. While she entered with warmth into these sports, being the soul of every festive party, her heart was consecrated to the promotion of happiness in every way in her power. When a child, playing with the little negresses of Martinique, she was adored as their queen. When in penury, crossing the Atlantic, by kind sympathy manifested for the sick and the sorrowful, she won the hearts of the seamen. When a prisoner, under sentence of death, by her cheerfulness, her forgetfulness of self, and her hourly deeds of delicate attention to others, she became an object of universal love in those cells of despair. When prosperity again dawned upon her, and she was in the enjoyment of an ample competence, every cottage in the vicinity of Malmaison testified to her benevolence. And now, when placed in a position of power, all her influence was exerted to relieve the misfortunes of those illustrious men whom the storms of revolution had driven from their homes and from France. She never forgot the unfortunate, but devoted a considerable portion of her income to the relief of the emigrants. She was at times accused of extravagance. Her nature was generous in the extreme, and the profusion of her expenditures was an index of her expansive benevolence.

Napoleon, soon after he became first consul, published a decree, inviting the emigrants to return, and did what he could to restore to them their confiscated estates. There were, however, necessarily exceptions from the general act of amnesty. Cases were continually arising of peculiar perplexity and hardship, where widows and orphans, reduced from opulence to penury, sought lost property, which, during the tumult of the times, had become involved in inextricable embarrassments. All such persons made application to Josephine. She ever found time to listen to their tales of sorrow, to speak words of sympathy, and, with great soundness of judgment, to render them all the aid in her power. "Josephine," said Napoleon, in reference to these her applications for the unfortunate, "will not take a refusal. But, it must be confessed, she rarely undertakes a case which has not propriety, at least, on its side." The Jacobin laws had fallen with fearful severity upon all the members of the ancient aristocracy and all the friends of royalty. The cause of these victims of anarchy Josephine was ever ready to espouse.

A noble family by the name of Decrest had been indebted to the interposition of the wife of the first consul for their permission to return to France. As nearly all their property had disappeared during their exile, Josephine continued to befriend them with her influence and her purse. On the evening of a festival day, a grand display of fire-works was exhibited on the banks of the Seine. A rocket, misdirected, struck a son of the marquis on the breast, and instantly killed him. The young man, who was on the eve of his marriage to the daughter of an ancient friend, was an officer of great promise, and the hope of the declining family. His death was a terrible calamity, as well as a most afflictive bereavement. The father abandoned himself to all the delirium of inconsolable grief, and was so utterly lost in the depths of despair, that it was feared his mind would never again recover its tone. The Duke of Orleans was grand-uncle of the young man who was killed, and Madame Montesson, the mother of Louis Philippe, sent for her distressed relatives that she might administer to their consolation. All her endeavors, however, were entirely unavailing.

In the midst of this afflictive scene, Josephine entered the saloon of Madame Montesson. Her own heart taught her that in such a grief as this words were valueless. Silently she took by the hand the eldest daughter, a beautiful girl, whose loveliness plead loudly for a father's care, and in the other arm she took their infant child of fifteen months, and, with her own cheeks bathed in tears, she kneeled before the stricken mourner. He raised his eyes and saw Josephine, the wife of the first consul, kneeling before him, and imploringly presenting his two children. He was at first astonished at the sight. Then, bursting into tears, he exclaimed, "Yes! I have much for which I am yet bound to live. These children have claims upon me, and I must no longer yield to despair." A lady who was present on this occasion says, "I witnessed this scene, and shall never forget it. The wife of the first consul expressed, in language which I will not attempt to imitate, all that tenderness which the maternal bosom alone knows. She was the very image of a ministering angel, for the touching charm of her voice and look pertained more to heaven than to earth." Josephine had herself seen days as dark as could lower over a mortal's path. Love for her children was then the only tie which bound her to life. In those days of anguish she learned the only appeal which, under these circumstances, could touch a despairing father's heart.

Several conspiracies were formed about this time against the life of the first consul. That of the Infernal Machine was one of the most desperate, reckless, and atrocious which history has recorded. On the evening of December 24, 1800, Napoleon was going to the opera. Three gentlemen were with him in his carriage. Josephine, with Hortense and one or two others, followed in another carriage. In passing from the Tuilleries to the theater, it was necessary to pass through the narrow street St. Nicaire. A cart, apparently by accident overturned, obstructed the passage. The coachman, however, who was driving his horses very rapidly, crowded his way by. He had barely passed the cart when a terrific explosion took place, which was heard all over Paris. Eight persons were instantly killed and more than sixty wounded. Some of the houses in the vicinity were nearly blown down. The windows of both the carriages were shattered, and Hortense was slightly wounded by the broken glass. Napoleon drove on to the opera, where he found the audience in the utmost consternation, for the explosion had shaken the whole city. He entered with a countenance as perfectly calm and untroubled as if nothing unusual had occurred. Every eye was fixed upon him. As soon as it was perceived that his person was safe, thunders of applause shook the walls of the theater. On every side Napoleon was greeted with the most devoted expressions of attachment. Soon Josephine came in, pale and trembling, and, after remaining half an hour, they both retired to the Tuilleries. Napoleon found the palace crowded with all the public functionaries of Paris, who had assembled to congratulate him upon his escape.

The life of Josephine was saved on this occasion by apparently the merest accident. She had recently received a magnificent shawl, a present from Constantinople, and was preparing to wear it that evening for the first time. Napoleon, however, in playful criticism, condemned the shawl, remarking upon its pattern and its color, and commending one which he deemed far more beautiful. "You are a bold man," said Josephine, smiling, "in venturing to criticise my toilette. I shall take my revenge in giving you a lesson how to attack a redoubt. However," she continued, turning to one of her attendants, "bring me the general's favorite. I will wear that." A delay of a few moments was caused in exchanging the shawls. In the mean time, Napoleon, with his friends, entered his carriage and drove on. Josephine soon followed. She had but just entered the street when the explosion took place. Had she followed, as usual, directly behind Napoleon, her death would have been almost inevitable.

It was subsequently ascertained, greatly to the surprise of Napoleon and of all Europe, that the Royalists were the agents in this conspiracy.

Napoleon had been their benefactor, and while he knew it to be impossible to replace the Bourbons upon the throne of France, he did every thing in his power to mitigate the misfortunes which Jacobin violence had inflicted upon their friends. The first consul made no disguise of his utter detestation of the Jacobins, and of their reign of merciless tyranny. He consequently supposed that they were the authors of the atrocious crime. The real authors of the conspiracy were however, soon discovered. Fouché, whom Bonaparte disliked exceedingly for his inhuman deeds during the Revolution, was the Minister of Police. Upon him mainly devolved the trial and the punishment of the accused. Josephine immediately wrote a letter to Fouché, most strikingly indicative of the benevolence of her noble heart, and of that strength of mind which could understand that the claims of justice must not pass unheeded.

"Citizen-Minister,—

While I yet tremble at the frightful event which has just occurred, I am disquieted and distressed through fear of the punishment necessarily to be inflicted on the guilty, who belong, it is said, to families with whom I once lived in habits of intercourse. I shall be solicited by mothers, sisters, and disconsolate wives; and my heart will be broken through my inability to obtain all the mercy for which I would plead.

"I know that the clemency of the first consul is great, his attachment to me extreme; but the crime is too dreadful that terrible examples should not be necessary. The chief of the government has not been alone exposed; and it is that which will render him severe—inflexible. I conjure you, therefore, to do all in your power to prevent inquiries being pushed too far. Do not detect all those persons who may have been accomplices in these odious transactions. Let not France, so long overwhelmed in consternation by public executions, groan anew beneath such inflictions. It is even better to endeavor to soothe the public mind than to exasperate men by fresh terrors. In short, when the ring-leaders of this nefarious attempt shall have been secured, let severity give place to pity for inferior agents, seduced as they may have been by dangerous falsehoods or exaggerated opinions.

"When just invested with supreme power, the first consul, as seems to me, ought rather to gain hearts than to be exhibited as ruling slaves. Soften by your counsels whatever may be too violent in his just resentment. Punish—alas! that you must certainly do—but pardon still more. Be also the support of those unfortunate men who, by frank avowal or repentance, shall expiate a portion of their crime.

"Having myself narrowly escaped perishing in the Revolution, you must regard as quite natural my interference on behalf of those who can be saved without involving in new danger the life of my husband, precious to me and to France. On this account, do, I entreat you, make a wide distinction between the authors of the crime and those who, through weakness or fear, have consented to take a part therein. As a woman, a wife, and a mother, I must feel the heart-rendings of those who will apply to me. Act, citizen minister, in such a manner that the number of these may be lessened. This will spare me much grief. Never will I turn away from the supplications of misfortune. But in the present instance you can do infinitely more than I, and you will, on this account, excuse my importunity. Rely on my gratitude and esteem."

Hortense was now eighteen years of age. Louis Napoleon, brother of the first consul, was twenty-four. The plan was formed by Napoleon and Josephine of uniting them in marriage. Louis was a studious, imaginative, pensive man, with no taste for the glitter and pomp of fashion, and with a decided aversion to earth's noisy ambition. He loved communing with his own thoughts, the falling leaf, the sighing wind—the fireside with its books, its solitude, its sacred society of one or two congenial friends. He belonged to that class of men, always imbued with deep feeling, whose happiness is only found in those hallowed affections which bind kindred hearts in congenial pursuits and joys. As Napoleon was riding triumphantly upon his war-horse over the Austrian squadrons in Italy, achieving those brilliant victories which paved his way to the throne of France, Louis, then a young man but nineteen years of age, met in Paris a young lady, the daughter of an emigrant noble, for whom he formed a strong attachment, and his whole soul became absorbed in the passion of love. Napoleon was informed of this attachment, and, apprehensive that the alliance of his brother with one of the old Royalist families might endanger his own ambitious projects, he sent him away on a military commission, and with his inflexible will and strong arm broke off the connection. The young lady was soon afterward married to another gentleman, and poor Louis was plunged into depths of disappointment and melancholy, from whence he never emerged. Life was ever after to him but a cloudy day, till, with a grief-worn spirit, he sank into the grave.

Napoleon, conscious of the wound he had inflicted upon his sensitive brother, endeavored, in various ways, to make amends. There was very much in his gentle, affectionate, and fervent spirit to attract the tender regard of Napoleon, and he ever after manifested toward him a disposition of peculiar kindness. It was long before Louis would listen to the proposition of his marriage with Hortense. His affections still clung, though hopelessly, yet so tenaciously to the lost object of his idolatry, that he could not think, without pain, of his union with another. More uncongenial nuptials could hardly have been imagined. Hortense was a beautiful, merry, thoughtless girl—amiable, but very fond of excitement and display. In the ball-room, the theater, and other places of brilliant entertainment, she found her chief pleasures. In addition to this incongruity, she was already in love with the handsome Duroc, the favorite aid of Napoleon. It is not strange that such a young lady should have seen as little to fancy in the disappointed and melancholy Louis as he could see attractive in one who lived but for the pageantry of the passing hour. Thus both parties were equally averse to the match. The tact of Josephine, however, and the power of Napoleon combined, soon overcame all obstacles, and the mirth-loving maiden and the pensive scholar were led to their untoward nuptials. Hortense became more easily reconciled to the match, as her powerful father promised, in consequence of this alliance, to introduce her to seats of grandeur where all her desires should be gratified. Louis, resigning himself to any lot in a world which had no further joy in store for him, suffered himself to be conducted submissively to the altar.

At the fête given in honor of this marriage, the splendors of ancient royalty seemed to be revived. But every eye could see the sadness of the newly-married bride beneath the profusion of diamonds and flowers with which she was adorned. Louis Napoleon, the present President of the French Republic, is the only surviving offspring of this uncongenial union.

The gay and handsome Duroc, who had been the accepted lover of Hortense, was soon after married to an heiress, who brought him, with an immense fortune, a haughty spirit and an irritable temper, which embittered all his days. The subsequent life of Hortense presents one of the most memorable illustrations of the insufficiency of human grandeur to promote happiness. Josephine witnessed with intense solicitude the utter want of congeniality existing between them, and her heart often bled as she saw alienation growing stronger and stronger, until it resulted in an entire separation. Hortense might easily have won and retained the affections of the pensive but warm-hearted Louis, had she followed the counsels of her noble mother. Josephine, herself the almost perfect model of a wife, was well qualified to give advice in such a case. The following letter, written to Hortense some time before her separation from Louis, exhibits in a most amiable light the character of Josephine.

THE HISTORY OF JOSEPHINE

To Queen Hortense.

"What I learned eight days ago gave me the greatest pain. What I observe to-day confirms and augments my sorrow. Why show to Louis this repugnance? Instead of rendering him more ungracious still by caprice, by inequality of character, why do you not rather make efforts to surmount your indifference? But you will say, he is not amiable! All that is relative. If not in your eyes amiable, he may appear so to others, and all women do not view him through the medium of dislike. As for myself, who am here altogether disinterested, I imagine that I behold him as he is, more *loving*, doubtless, than *lovable*, but this is a great and rare quality. He is generous, beneficent, feeling, and, above all, an excellent father. If you so willed, he would prove a good husband. His melancholy, his love of study and retirement, injure him in your estimation. For these, I ask you, is he to blame? Is he obliged to conform his nature to circumstances? Who could have predicted to him his fortune? But, according to you, he has not even the *courage* to bear that fortune. This, I believe, is an error; but he certainly wants the *strength*. With his ascetic inclinations, his invincible desire of retirement and study, he finds himself misplaced in the elevated rank to which he has attained. You desire that he should imitate his brother. Give him, first of all, the same temperament. You have not failed to remark that almost our entire existence depends upon our health, and that upon our digestion. Let poor Louis digest better, and you would find him more amiable. But, such as he is, there can be no reason for abandoning him, or making him feel the unbecoming sentiments with which he inspires you. Do you, whom I have seen so kind, continue to be so at the moment when it is precisely more than ever necessary. Take pity on a man who has to lament that he possesses what would constitute another's happiness; and, before condemning him, think of others who, like him, have groaned beneath the burden of their greatness, and bathed with their tears that diadem which they believed had never been destined for their brow."

This, surely, was admirable counsel, and, had Hortense followed it, she would have saved herself many a long year of loneliness and anguish. But the impetuous and thoughtless bride could not repress the repugnance with which she regarded the cold exterior and the exacting love of her husband. Louis demanded from her a singleness and devotedness of affection which was unreasonable. He wished to engross all her faculties of loving. He desired that every passion of her soul should be centered in him, and was jealous of any happiness she found excepting that which he could give. He was even troubled by the tender regard with which she cherished her mother and her brother, considering all the love she gave to them as so much withheld from him. Hortense was passionately fond of music and of painting. Louis almost forbade her the enjoyment of those delightful accomplishments, thinking that she pursued them with a heartfelt devotion inconsistent with that supreme love with which she ought to regard her husband. Hortense, proud and high-spirited, would not submit to such tyranny. She resisted and retaliated. She became, consequently, wretched, and her husband wretched, and discord withered all the joys of home. At last, the union of such discordant spirits became utterly insupportable. They separated. The story of their domestic quarrels vibrated upon the ear of Europe. Louis wandered here and there, joyless and sad, till, weary of a miserable life, alone and friendless, he died. Hortense retired, with a restless and suffering heart, to the mountains of Switzerland, where, in a secluded castle, she lingered out the remaining years of her sorrowful pilgrimage. It was an unfortunate match. Having been made, the only possible remedy was in pursuing the course which Josephine so earnestly recommended. Had Josephine been married to Louis, she would have followed the course she counseled her daughter to pursue. She would have leaned fondly upon his arm in his morning and evening walks. She would have cultivated a lively interest in his reading, his studies, and all his quiet domestic pleasures. She would, as far as possible, have relinquished every pursuit which could by any possibility have caused him pain. Thus she would have won his love and his admiration. Every day her power over him would have been increasing. Gradually her influence would have molded his character to a better model. He would have become proud of his wife. He would have leaned upon her arm. He would have been supported by her affection and her intellectual strength. He would have become more cheerful in character and resolute in purpose. Days of tranquillity and happiness would have embellished their dwelling. The spirit of Josephine! It is *noble* as well as *lovely*. It accomplishes the most exalted achievements, and diffuses the most ennobling happiness. There are thousands of unions as uncongenial as that of Hortense and Louis. From the woes such unions would naturally engender there is but one refuge, and Josephine has most beautifully shown what that refuge is. Hortense, proud and high-spirited, resolved that she would not submit to the exacting demands of her husband. In her sad fate we read the warning not to imitate her example.

Hortense is invariably described as an unusually fascinating woman. She had great vivacity of mind, and displayed much brilliance of conversational powers. Her person was finely formed, and she inherited much of that graceful demeanor which so signally characterized her mother. She was naturally amiable, and was richly endowed with all those accomplishments which enable one to excel in the art of pleasing. Louis, more than any other of the brothers, most strongly resembled Napoleon. He was a very handsome man, and possessed far more than ordinary abilities. Under less untoward circumstances he might have been eminently happy. Few persons, however, have journeyed along the path of life under a darker cloud than that which ever shed its gloom upon the footsteps of Louis and Hortense.

Among the various attempts which had been made to produce alienation between Napoleon and Josephine, one of the most atrocious was the whispered insinuation that the strong affection which the first consul manifested for Hortense was a guilty passion. Napoleon exhibited in the most amiable manner his qualities as a father, in the frequent correspondence he carried on with the two children of Josephine, in the interest he took in their studies, and in the solicitude he manifested to promote their best welfare. He loved Hortense as if she had been his own child. Josephine was entirely impregnable against any jealousy to be introduced from that quarter, and a peaceful smile was her only reply to all such insinuations. Hortense had also heard, and had utterly disregarded, these rumors. The marriage of Hortense to a brother of Napoleon had entirely silenced the calumny, and it was soon forgotten.

Subsequently, when Hortense had become entirely alienated from her husband, and was resolved upon a separation, Josephine did every thing in her power to dissuade her from an act so rash, so disgraceful, so ruinous to her happiness. She wrote to her in terms of the most earnest entreaty. The self-willed queen, annoyed by these remonstrances, and unable to reply to them, ventured to intimate to her mother that perhaps she was not entirely disinterested in her opposition. In most guarded terms she suggested that her mother had heard the groundless accusation of Napoleon's undue fondness, and that it was possible that her strong opposition to the separation of Hortense from her husband might originate in the fear that Hortense might become, in some degree, her rival in the affections of Napoleon. Josephine very promptly and energetically replied,

> "You have misunderstood me entirely, my child. There is nothing equivocal in my words, as there can not exist an uncandid sentiment in my heart. How could you imagine that I could participate in opinions so ridiculous and so malicious? No, Hortense, you do not think that I believe you to be my rival. We do, indeed, both reign in the same heart, though by very different, yet by equally sacred rights. And they who, in the affection which my husband manifests for you, have pretended to discover other sentiments than those of a parent and a friend, know not *his* soul. His mind

is too elevated above that of the vulgar to be ever accessible to unworthy passions. The passion of glory, if you will, engrosses him too entirely for our repose; but glory, at least, inspires nothing which is vile. Such is my profession of faith respecting Napoleon. I make this confession to you in all sincerity, that I may allay your inquietudes. When I recommended you to love, or, at least, not to repulse Louis, I spoke to you in my character of an experienced wife, an attentive mother, and a tender friend, and in this threefold relation do I now embrace you."

10

The Coronation

A.D. 1800-A.D. 1804

Early in the year 1802 Josephine accompanied Napoleon in various excursions to distant parts of the empire. She went with him to Lyons to meet the Italian deputies, who had assembled there to confer upon him the dignity of President of the Cisalpine Republic. The entertainments in Lyons upon this occasion were arranged with regal magnificence. Josephine, by her grace and affability, secured universal admiration, and every tongue was eloquent in her praises. Each succeeding month seemed now to bring some new honor to Josephine. Her position as wife of the first consul, her known influence over her husband, and the almost boundless popularity he had acquired over the minds of his countrymen, who were ever conducting him by rapid strides to new accessions of power, surrounded her with multitudes striving in every way to ingratiate themselves into her favor.

From Lyons they returned to their beloved retreat at Malmaison, where they passed several weeks. But place and power had already deprived them of retirement. Napoleon was entirely engrossed with his vast projects of ambition. The avenue to their rural mansion was unceasingly thronged with carriages, and the saloon of Josephine was ever filled with the most illustrious guests.

One day Josephine happened to be in the cabinet with her husband alone. A man, whose coat was much the worse for wear, and whose whole appearance presented many indications of the struggle with poverty, was ushered into the room. He appeared greatly embarrassed, and at length, with much confusion, introduced himself as the writing-master at Brienne who had taught the first consul hand-writing. "And a fine penman you made of me!" exclaimed Napoleon, in affected anger. "Ask my wife there what she thinks of my writing." The poor man stood trembling in trepidation, when Josephine looked up with one of her sweetest smiles, and said, "I assure you, sir, his letters are perfectly delightful." Napoleon laughed at the well-timed compliment, and settled upon the writing-master a small annuity for life. It was a noble trait in the character of the first consul that in his days of power he was ever mindful of those who were the friends of his early years. All the instructors of the school he attended at Brienne were thus remembered by him.

Napoleon and Josephine now made the tour of the northern provinces of France. They were every where received with unbounded enthusiasm. The first consul had, indeed, conferred the greatest blessings on his country. He had effectually curbed the Revolutionary fury. He had established the reign of law. Thousands of exiles he had restored to their homes rejoicing. The discomfited armies of France he had led to new and brilliant victories. Under his administration every branch of business had revived. From every part of the empire Napoleon received the most enthusiastic expressions of gratitude and attachment. He now began more seriously to contemplate ascending the throne of France. Conscious of his own power, and ambitious of the glory of elevating his country to the highest pinnacle of earthly greatness, and witnessing the enthusiasm of admiration which his deeds had excited in the public mind, he no longer doubted that his countrymen would soon be ready to place the scepter of empire in his hands. He thought that the pear was now ripe.

Josephine ever enjoyed most highly accompanying her husband on these tours, and she, on such occasions, manifested, in the most attractive manner, her readiness to sacrifice her own personal comfort to promote the happiness of others. Napoleon was in the habit of moving with such rapidity, and of setting out so unexpectedly upon these journeys, and he was so peremptory in his injunctions as to the places where he intended to halt, that often no suitable accommodations could be provided for Josephine and her attendant ladies. No complaint, however, was ever heard from her lips. No matter how great the embarrassment she encountered, she ever exhibited the same imperturbable cheerfulness and good humor. She always manifested much more solicitude in reference to the accommodation of her attendants than for her own comfort. She would herself visit their apartments, and issue personal directions to promote their convenience. One night, just as she was about to retire to rest, she observed that her waiting-woman had but a single mattress, spread upon the floor, for her repose. She immediately, with her own hands, took from the bed destined for herself another mattress, and supplied the deficiency, that her waiting-woman might sleep more comfortably. Whenever any of her household were sick, Josephine promptly visited their bed-side, and with her own hands ministered to their wants. She would remember them at her own table, and from the luxurious viands spread out before her, would select delicacies which might excite a failing appetite. It often happened, in these sudden and hasty journeys, that, from want of accommodation, some of the party were compelled to remain in the carriages while Napoleon and Josephine dined. In such cases they were never forgotten. This was not policy and artifice on the part of Josephine, but the instinctive dictates of a heart overflowing with benevolence.

On Napoleon's return from this tour he took possession of the palace of St. Cloud. This was another step toward the throne of the Bourbons. This magnificent abode of ancient grandeur had been repaired and most gorgeously furnished. The versatile French, weary of Republican simplicity, witnessed with joy the indications of a return of regal magnificence. A decree also granted to Josephine "four ladies, to assist her in doing the honors of the palace." No occupant of these splendid saloons ever embellished them more richly by the display of queenly graces than did Josephine; and Napoleon, now constituted first consul for life, reigned with pomp and power which none of his predecessors had ever surpassed. The few remaining forms of the Republic rapidly disappeared. Josephine exerted much influence over her husband's mind in inducing him to re-establish the institutions of the Christian religion. Napoleon at that time did not profess to have any faith in the divine origin of Christianity. Infidelity had swept resistlessly over France, and nearly every man of any note in the camp and in the court was an unbeliever. He was, consequently, very bitterly opposed in all his endeavors to reinstate Christianity. One evening he was walking upon the terrace of his garden at Malmaison, most earnestly conversing with some influential members of the government upon this subject.

"Religion," said he, "is something which can not be eradicated from the heart of man. He *must* believe in a superior being. Who made all that?" he continued, pointing to the stars brilliantly shining in the evening sky. "Last Sunday evening I was walking here alone, when the church bells of the village of Ruel rang at sunset. I was strongly moved, so vividly did the image of early days come back with that sound. If it be thus with me, what must it be with others? Let your philosophers answer that, if they can. It is absolutely indispensable to have a religion for the people. In re-establishing Christianity, I consult the wishes of a great majority of the French nation."

Josephine probably had very little religious knowledge. She regarded Christianity as a sentiment rather than a principle. She felt the poetic beauty of its revelations and its ordinances. She knew how holy were its charities, how pure its precepts, how ennobling its influences, even when encumbered with the grossest superstitions. She had seen, and dreadfully had she felt, what France was without religion—with marriage a mockery, conscience a phantom, and death proclaimed to all an eternal sleep. She therefore most warmly seconded her husband in all endeavors to restore again to desolated France the religion of Jesus Christ.

The next morning after the issuing of the proclamation announcing the re-establishment of public worship, a grand religious ceremony took place in honor of the occasion in the church of Nôtre Dame. Napoleon, to produce a deep impression upon the public mind, invested the occasion with all possible pomp. As he was preparing to go to the Cathedral, one of his colleagues, Cambacérès, entered the room.

"Well," said the first consul, rubbing his hands in fine spirits, "we go to church this morning; what say they to that in Paris?"

"Many people," replied Cambacérès, "propose to attend the first representation in order to hiss the piece, should they not find it amusing."

"If any one takes it into his head to hiss, I shall put him out of the door by the grenadiers of the consular guard."

"But what if the grenadiers themselves take to hissing like the rest?"

"As to that, I have no fear. My old mustaches will go here to Nôtre Dame just as at Cairo they would have gone to the mosque. They will remark how I do, and, seeing their general grave and decent, they will be so too, passing the watchword to each other, *Decency*!"

In the noble proclamation which the first consul issued upon this great event, he says, "An insane policy has sought, during the Revolution, to smother religious dissensions under the ruins of the altar, under the ashes of religion itself. At its voice all those pious solemnities ceased in which the citizens called each other by the endearing name of brothers, and acknowledged their common equality in the sight of Heaven. The dying, left alone in his agonies, no longer heard that consoling voice which calls the Christian to a better world. God himself seemed exiled from the face of nature. Ministers of the religion of peace! let a complete oblivion veil over your dissensions, your misfortunes, your faults. Let the religion which unites you bind you by indissoluble cords to the interests of your country. Citizens of the Protestant faith! the law has equally extended its solicitude to your interests. Let the morality, so pure, so holy, so brotherly, which you profess, unite you all in love

THE HISTORY OF JOSEPHINE

to your country and respect for its laws; and, above all, never permit disputes on doctrinal points to weaken that universal charity which religion at once inculcates and commands."

This, surely, is a great triumph of Christianity. A man like Napoleon, even though not at the time a believer in its divine origin, was so perfectly satisfied of its beneficial influence upon mankind, that, as a matter of state policy, he felt compelled to reinstate its observances.

Josephine cherished emotions of the deepest gratitude toward all those who had proved friendly to her in the days of her adversity. Napoleon, with his strong prejudices, often took a dislike to those whom Josephine loved. Madame Tallien, the companion of Josephine in her captivity and her benefactor after her release, was, for some unknown reason, peculiarly obnoxious to Napoleon. She was extremely beautiful and very ambitious, and her exclusion from the splendors of the new court, now daily becoming more brilliant, mortified her exceedingly. Josephine also was greatly troubled. She could not disregard the will of her husband, and her heart recoiled from the thought of ingratitude toward one who had been her friend in adversity. At this time, in Paris, pleasure seemed to be the universal object of pursuit. All the restraints of religion had been swept away, and masked balls, gambling, and every species of dissipation attracted to the metropolis the wealthy and the dissolute from all parts of Europe. Napoleon never made his appearance in any of these reckless scenes of revelry. He ever was an inveterate enemy to gambling in all its forms, and had no relish for luxurious indulgence. Josephine, however, accompanied by Eugene, occasionally looked in upon the dancers at the masked balls. On one of these occasions a noble lady witnessed an incident which she has recorded in the following words:

> "Chance rendered me witness of a singular scene at one of these balls. It was near two o'clock in the morning, the crowd immense, and the heat overpowering. I had ascended for a few moments to the apartments above, and, refreshed by the cool air, was about

to descend, when the sound of voices in the adjoining room, in earnest conversation, caught my attention. Applying my ear to the partition, the name of Bonaparte, and the discovery that Josephine and Madame Tallien were the speakers, excited a real curiosity. 'I assure you, my dear Theresina,' said Josephine, 'that I have done all that friendship could dictate, but in vain. No later than this morning I made a new effort. Bonaparte would hear of nothing. I can not comprehend what can have prejudiced him so strongly against you. You are the only woman whose name he has effaced from the list of my particular friends; and from fear lest he should manifest his displeasure directly against us have I now come hither alone with my son. At this moment they believe me sound asleep in my bed at the Tuilleries; but I determined on coming to see, to warn, and to console you and, above all, to justify myself.'

"'My dear Josephine,' Madame Tallien replied, 'I have never doubted either the goodness of your heart or the sincerity of your affection. Heaven is my witness that the loss of your friendship would be to me much more painful than any dread of Bonaparte. In these difficult times, I have maintained a conduct that might, perhaps, render my visits an honor, but I will never importune you to receive me without his consent. He was not consul when Tallien followed him into Egypt, when I received you both into my house, when I shared with you—' Here she burst into tears, and her voice became inaudible.

"'Calm yourself, my dear Theresina,' Josephine rejoined; 'be calm, and let the storm pass. I am paving the way for a reconciliation, but we must not irritate him more. You know that he does not love Ouvrard, and it is said that he often sees you.'

"'What, then,' Madame Tallien replied, 'because he governs France, does he expect to tyrannize over our hearts? Must we sacrifice to him our private friendships?' Eugene interrupts it.

"At that moment some one knocked at the door, and Eugene Beauharnais entered. 'Madame,' said he to his mother, 'you have been now more than an hour absent. The council of ministers is perhaps over. What will the first consul say, should he not find you on his return?' The two ladies then, arm in arm, descended the stairs, conversing in earnest whispers, followed by Eugene."

This Ouvrard, to whom allusion is made above, was a famous banker in Paris, of enormous wealth, and engaged in the most wild and extravagant speculations.

It now began to be rumored that Napoleon would soon be crowned as king. Very many of the nation desired it, and though there was as yet no public declaration, vague hints and floating rumors filled the air. Josephine was greatly disquieted. It seemed more and more important that Napoleon should have an heir. There was now no prospect that Josephine would ever become again a mother. She heard, with irrepressible anguish, that it had been urged upon her husband that the interests of France required that he should obtain a divorce and marry again; that alliance with one of the ancient royal families of Europe, and the birth of a son, to whom he could transmit his crown, would place his power upon an impregnable foundation. Josephine could not but perceive the *apparent* policy of the great wrong. And though she knew that Napoleon truly and tenderly loved her, she also feared that there was no sacrifice which he was not ready to make in obedience to the claims of his towering ambition.

One day she softly entered the cabinet without being announced. Bonaparte and Bourrienne were conversing together. The day before, an article appeared in the Moniteur, evidently preparing the way for the throne. Josephine gently approached her husband, sat down upon his knee, affectionately passed her hand through his hair and over his face, and, with moistened eyes and a burst of tenderness, exclaimed, "I entreat you, mon ami, do not make yourself a king. It is Lucien who urges you to it. Do not even listen to him."

Bonaparte, smiling very pleasantly, replied, "Why, my dear Josephine, you are crazy. You must not listen to these tales of the old dowagers. But you interrupt us now. I am very busy."

During the earlier period of Napoleon's consulship, like the humblest citizen, he occupied the same bed-chamber with his spouse. But now that more of regal ceremony and state was being introduced to the consular establishment, their domestic intercourse, to the great grief of Josephine, assumed more of cold formality. Separate apartments were assigned to Josephine at a considerable distance from those occupied by her husband, and it was necessary to traverse a long corridor to pass from one to the other. The chambers of the principal ladies of the court opened upon this corridor from the right and the left. The splendor with which Josephine's rooms were furnished was no compensation to her for the absence of that affectionate familiarity for which her heart ever yearned. She also suspected, with anguish, that this separation was but the prelude of the divorce she so fearfully apprehended. Whenever Napoleon passed the night in the apartment of Josephine, it was known to the whole household. Josephine, at such times, always appeared at a later hour in the morning than usual, for they generally passed half the night in conversation.

"I think I see her still," writes one of the ladies of her household, "coming in to breakfast, looking quite cheerful, rubbing her little hands, as she was accustomed to do when peculiarly happy, and apologizing for having risen so late. On such occasions she was, if possible, more gracious than usual, refused nobody, and we were sure of obtaining every thing we asked, as I have myself many times experienced."

The Bourbons had been for some time in correspondence with Napoleon, hoping, through his agency, to regain the throne. He assured them that their restoration could not possibly be accomplished, even by the sacrifice of the lives of a million of Frenchmen. Josephine, who had suffered so much from anarchy, was a decided Royalist, and she exerted all her powers to induce Napoleon to make the attempt to reinstate the Bourbons. When her friends congratulated her upon the probability that she would soon be Empress of France, with heartfelt sincerity she replied, "To be the wife of the first consul fulfills my highest ambition. Let me remain so." The Bourbons expressed much gratitude at the time in view of Josephine's known intercessions in their behalf.

About this time a serious accident happened to the first consul, which also exposed Josephine to much danger. The inhabitants of Antwerp had made Napoleon a present of six magnificent bay horses. With four of these spirited steeds harnessed to the carriage, Napoleon was one day taking an airing, with Josephine and Cambacérès, the second consul, in the park. Napoleon, taking a fancy to drive four in hand, mounted the coach-box, and Cæsar, his favorite coachman, was stationed behind. The horses soon discovered that they had a new and inexperienced driver, and started off at the top of their speed. Napoleon lost all control over them, and the frightened animals, perfectly ungovernable, dashed along the road at a fearful rate. Cæsar kept shouting to Napoleon, "Keep in the middle!" Cambacérès, pale with fright, thrust his head out of the window, and shouted "Whoa! whoa!" Josephine, greatly alarmed, sank back in her seat, and in silent resignation awaited the issue. As they approached the avenue to St. Cloud, the imperial driver had not sufficient skill to guide them safely through the gateway. The coach struck against one of the pillars, and was overturned with a terrible crash. Josephine and Cambacérès were considerably bruised. Napoleon was thrown from his seat to the distance of eight or ten paces, and was taken up insensible. He, however, soon recovered. On retiring at night, they amused themselves in talking over the misadventure. "Mon ami," said Josephine, laughing, "you must render unto Cæsar the things that be Cæsar's. Let him keep his whip. Each to his vocation." The conversation was continued for some time in a tone of pleasantry. Gradually Napoleon became more serious. He seemed to be reflecting deeply, and said that he never before came so near to death. "Indeed," said he, "I was for some moments virtually dead. But what is death? what is death? It is merely a sleep without dreams."

Such were probably, at this time, the views of Napoleon upon immortality. He subsequently professed himself a sincere believer in the divine origin of Christianity, and wished to die within the pale of the Christian Church. That mind which can contemplate death with levity must be either exceedingly weak or hopelessly deranged.

While nearly all who surrounded the first consul were contemplating with the utmost satisfaction his approaching elevation to the throne, the subject awakened in the bosom of Josephine the most agitating emotions. She saw in the splendor of the throne peril to her husband, and the risk of entire downfall to herself. "The real enemies of Bonaparte," said she to Rœderer, "are those who put into his head ideas of hereditary succession, dynasty, divorce, and marriage." Again she is represented as saying, "I do not approve the projects of Napoleon. I have often told him so. He hears me with attention, but I can plainly see that I make no impression. The flatterers who surround him soon obliterate all that I have said. The new honors which he will acquire will augment the number of his enemies. The generals will exclaim that they have not fought so long merely to substitute the family of the Bonapartes for that of the Bourbons."

The peace ratified by the treaty of Amiens in 1802 threw open the Continent to travelers from England. There were thousands in that country who were great admirers of Napoleon. The Tuilleries, St. Cloud, and Malmaison were consequently ever thronged with illustrious strangers from the island with which France had so long been engaged in war. The celebrated statesman, Mr. Fox, with Lord and Lady Holland, Lord Erskine, and several others of the most distinguished of the English nobility, were visiting Paris, and one morning were at a breakfast party at Madame Recamier's. Breakfast was nearly concluded, when the sounds of a horseman galloping into the court-yard were heard. Eugene Beauharnais was immediately after announced. After a few words of regret expressed to the lady of the house for having arrived so late, he turned to Mr. Fox and said, "I hope, sir, soon to indemnify myself for the loss of your society which I have this morning sustained. I am commissioned by my mother to attend you to Malmaison. The carriages will be here in a few moments which are for the accommodation of you and your friends, when you can resolve on leaving so many charms as must detain you here. I shall, with much pleasure, act as your guide."

The carriages of the first consul soon arrived, and the whole party proceeded to Malmaison. Josephine received her guests with that courtesy and refined cordiality in which she was unrivaled. Bonaparte, knowing the powerful influence of the illustrious English statesman, was very desirous that he should receive a favorable impression from his visit. It required but little effort on the part of Josephine to excel in the art of pleasing. She banished all parade, and received her guests as family friends. The day was spent at Malmaison, and Mr. Fox afterward stated that he retired from the visit enchanted with the elegance and grace of all that he saw and heard.

Ten years had passed, during which France had been in a state of constant warfare. The short peace which succeeded the treaty of Amiens filled Paris with the best society of Europe. Extravagance and dissipation reigned in the metropolis. But in those scenes of dissipation neither Napoleon nor Josephine ever made their appearance. His mind was ever engrossed with the magnificent plans he was forming and the deeds he was achieving. Josephine was equally engaged in watching over the interests of her husband, and in gaining and confirming friends to his cause.

On the 18th of May, 1804, by a decree of the senate, Napoleon was declared Emperor of France. The decree was sent out to the various departments for the action of the people. The result was, that 3,572,329 voted in the affirmative, while but 2569 were in the negative. A more unanimous expression of a nation's will history never has recorded. The day after his elevation to the imperial throne, the emperor held a grand levée at the Tuilleries, and Josephine, with many fears darkening this hour of exultation, made her first appearance as the Empress of France. The decree announcing Napoleon Bonaparte to be the emperor of France also declared that the imperial dignity should be *hereditary* in his family. The empress struggled against her fears, but her heart was heavy, and she found but little joy upon this high pinnacle of power. She also plainly foresaw that the throne of her husband, apparently so gorgeous and massive, was erected upon a very frail foundation.

At the grand levée held upon this occasion, the assembly was the most brilliant and numerous that had ever yet been witnessed in Paris. The renown of Napoleon now filled the world, and noted men from every land thronged his saloons. Josephine found herself elevated to the position of the most illustrious of the queens of Europe. The power of her husband was superior to that of any of the surrounding monarchs, and she received the homage of all as occupying an elevation such as no queen had ever attained before.

The second of December, 1804, was appointed for the ceremony of coronation. The pageant was to take place in the church of Nôtre Dame. The pope came from Rome to place the crown upon this lofty, though plebeian brow. For ten centuries such an honor had not been conferred upon any monarch. The day was clear and brilliant, but intensely cold. The venerable walls of Nôtre Dame had never before witnessed such luxury and such magnificence as was now displayed. Carriages glittering with gold and purple trappings; horses proudly caparisoned; officers in the richest uniforms, and in court dresses sumptuously embroidered; servants in most gorgeous liveries; and a waving sea of ostrich plumes, bewildered the multitude with the unwonted splendor.

The empress appeared in a robe of white satin, embroidered with gold, and profusely ornamented with diamonds. A mantle of crimson velvet, lined with white satin and ermine, floated over her shoulders, and golden bees were clustered over the dress. The coronation jewels consisted of a crown, a diadem, and a girdle. The coronation crown consisted of eight golden branches, four in imitation of palm, and four of myrtle leaves. The dew-drops glittering upon this foliage were brilliant diamonds. A golden-corded band surrounded the crown, embellished with eight very large emeralds. The bandeau inclosing the head glittered resplendent with amethysts. This was the coronation crown, which was used only upon state occasions. The diadem, which was for more ordinary service, was composed of four rows of pearls interlaced with diamonds. In front were several very large brilliants, one of which weighed one hundred and forty-nine grains. The ceinture or girdle was of pure gold, so pure as to be quite elastic, embellished with thirty-nine rose-colored diamonds.

Napoleon wore a close dress of white velvet, embroidered in gold, with diamond buttons. His stockings were of white silk. The robe and mantle were of crimson velvet, richly embroidered in gold and embellished with diamonds. Napoleon seemed to regret the vast expense attending this display, while at the same time he was conscious of its importance to impress the minds of the Parisians. The emperor was profuse in expenditure to promote the grandeur and glory of the nation, but very frugal in his personal expenses.

The imperial carriage, constructed expressly for the occasion, was the most exquisite piece of workmanship Parisian ingenuity could devise. It was drawn by eight bay horses. The paneling was entirely of glass. As the emperor and empress entered the carriage, they both, by mistake, sat down with their backs toward the horses. Josephine, immediately perceiving the error, lightly changed her seat, at the same time saying smilingly to her husband, as she pointed to the rich cushion at her side, "Mon ami! unless you prefer riding vis-à-vis, this is your seat." Napoleon laughed heartily at the blunder, and changed his seat. Double files of infantry lined the route of more than a mile and a half, extending from the Tuilleries to Nôtre Dame. Ten thousand horsemen, in most gorgeous uniforms, attended the carriages. Half a million of spectators thronged the way, crowding the windows and balconies, clustered upon the house-tops, and filling up every space from whence any view of the cortège could be gained. The air was filled with the martial strains of a thousand bands, with the thunders of innumerable pieces of artillery, and with the enthusiastic acclamations of the vast multitude. A pageant more sublime this world perhaps has never witnessed.

The Coronation.

The throne, which was hung with crimson velvet, was overarched with a canopy of the same rich material. It was ascended by twenty-two circular steps, which were covered with blue cloth, studded with golden bees. The most illustrious officers of the empire crowded the stairs. Napoleon and Josephine sat, side by side, upon the throne. The religious ceremony occupied nearly four hours. It was interspersed with the most soul-stirring music from martial bands and from more than three hundred vocal performers. When the pope was about to place the crown upon the brow of the emperor, Napoleon took it from him, and placed it, with his own hands, upon his head. He then took it off and crowned the empress, also with his own hands, fixing his eye proudly, yet most tenderly, upon her. The heavy crown was soon after laid upon a cushion, while a smaller diadem was placed upon the head of Josephine. She kneeled before her illustrious consort as he placed the crown of France upon her brow. After remaining for a moment in silence in the posture of prayer, with her hands folded over her bosom, she then gracefully rose, her eyes swimming in tears, and turned to her husband with a look of gratitude and of love which the emperor feelingly recognized. It was a touching scene, and in that moment were clustered the memories of years.

But the day was not without its moments of anguish for Josephine. In the brief speech which the emperor made upon the occasion, he said, "*My descendants will long sit upon this throne.*" These words were as a dagger to the heart of the empress. She knew Napoleon's intense desire for an heir. She knew how strong the desire in France was that he should have a son to whom to transmit his throne. She knew how much had been said respecting the necessity of a divorce. The most infamous proposals had been urged upon her by pretended friends, even by one of the brothers of Napoleon, that she might, by unfaithfulness to him, obviate the necessity of Napoleon's seeking another bride. This sentiment, uttered upon the day of coronation, filled her heart with fear and anguish.

The shades of evening had fallen upon the swarming city, and all the streets of the metropolis and the broad façade of the Tuilleries were glittering with illuminations when the emperor and empress returned to the palace. Josephine, overcome with the conflicting emotions which the day had excited, retired to her apartment, and, falling upon her knees, with tears implored the guidance of the King of kings. Napoleon hastened to his room, exclaiming impatiently to an attendant as he entered, "Off, off with these confounded trappings!" He threw the mantle into one corner of the room, and the gorgeous robe into another, and, thus violently disencumbering himself, declared that hours of such mortal tediousness he had never encountered before.

Josephine, in her remonstrances with Napoleon against assuming the crown, predicted, with almost prophetic accuracy, the consequences which would ensue. "Will not your power," she wrote to him, "opposed, as to a certainty it must be, by the neighboring states, draw you into a war with them? This will probably end in their ruin. Will not their neighbors, beholding these effects, combine for your destruction?

While abroad such is the state of things, at home how numerous the envious and discontented! How many plots to disconcert, and how many conspiracies to punish."

Soon after the coronation, Josephine was one morning in her garden, when an intimate friend called to see her. She saluted the empress by the title of Your Majesty. "Ah!" she exclaimed, in tones deeply pathetic, "I entreat that you will suffer me, at least here, to forget that I am an empress." It is the unvarying testimony of her friends, that, while she was receiving with surpassing gracefulness the congratulations of France and of Europe, her heart was heavy. She clearly foresaw the peril of their position, and trembled in view of an approaching downfall. The many formal ceremonies which her station required, and upon which Napoleon laid great stress, were exceedingly irksome to one whose warm heart rejoiced in the familiarity of unrestrained friendship. She thus described her feelings: "The nearer my husband approached the summit of earthly greatness, the more dim became my last gleams of happiness. It is true that I enjoyed a magnificent existence. My court was composed of gentlemen and ladies the most illustrious in rank, all of whom were emulous of the honor of being presented to me. But my time was no longer at my command. The emperor was receiving from every part of France congratulations upon his accession to the throne, while I myself sighed in contemplating the immense power he had acquired. The more I saw him loaded with the gifts of Fortune, the more I feared his fall."

The court of France had for ages been the scene of the most voluptuous and unblushing vice. The whole nation had been corrupted by its influence. Dissipation had been rendered attractive by the grace with which it had been robed. The dissolute manners which had prevailed at Versailles, the Tuilleries, and St. Cloud no pen can describe. Napoleon determined that, at all hazards, his court should be reputable at least in outward morality. He was more scrupulous upon this point even than Josephine herself. Believing that the downfall of the Bourbons was caused, in no inconsiderable degree, by the dissolute lives of the nobles

THE HISTORY OF JOSEPHINE

and the courtiers, he would give no one an appointment among the royal retinue whose character was not, in his judgment, above reproach.

The Duchess d'Aiguillon had been a fellow-captive of Josephine, and, after their liberation from prison, had greatly befriended her. During the license of those times, in which all the restraints of Christian morality had been swept away, her character had not remained perfectly spotless. She and her husband had availed themselves of the facile liberty of divorce which the laws had encouraged, and had formed other unions. Josephine felt grateful for the many favors she had received from the duchess, and wished to testify this gratitude by receiving her at court. Napoleon peremptorily refused. Josephine wrote to her in the following terms:

"My dear Friend,—

I am deeply afflicted. My former friends, supposing that I am able to obtain the fulfillment of all my wishes, must suppose that I have forgotten the past. Alas! it is not so. I remember it too well, and my thoughts dwell upon it more than I would have them. The more I think of what my friends did for me, the greater is my sorrow at being unable to do now what my heart dictates. The Empress of France is but the first slave in the empire, and can not pay the debts of Madame de Beauharnais. This constitutes the torture of my life, and will explain why you do not occupy a place near me. The emperor, indignant at the total disregard of morality, and alarmed at the progress it might still make, is resolved that the example of a life of regularity and of religion shall be presented in the palace where he reigns. Desirous of strengthening more and more the Church re-established by himself, and unable to change the laws appointed by her observances, his intention is, at least, to keep at a distance from his court all who may have availed themselves of the opportunity for a divorce. Hence the cause of his refusing the favor I asked of having you with me. The refusal has occasioned me unspeakable regret, but he is too absolute to leave even the hope of seeing him retract. I am thus constrained to renounce the pleasure I had promised myself of being constantly with you, studying to make you forget the sovereign in the friend. Pity my lot in being too public a personage to follow my own inclination, and cherish for me a friendship, the remembrance of which gives me now as much pleasure as its reality afforded consolation in prison. Often do I regret that small, dark, and dismal chamber which we shared together, for there, at least, I could pour out my whole heart, and was sincerely beloved in return."

11

Josephine and Empress

A.D. 1805

During the whole month succeeding the coronation, Paris was surrendered to fêtes, illuminations, and all manner of public rejoicing. One morning the empress found in her apartment, as a present from the municipality of the capital, a toilet service, with table, ewer, and basin of massive gold, wrought with most exquisite workmanship. An enormous balloon, in the form of the imperial crown, brilliantly illuminated, was launched, the evening of the coronation, from Paris. The vast structure, weighing five hundred pounds, floated most majestically over the city, for a time the object of the gaze of a million of eyes, till, borne away by the wind toward the south, it disappeared. The next evening it fell near the city of Rome, nine hundred miles from Paris. "Sire," said a courtier, announcing the fact to Napoleon, "your imperial crown has appeared in the two great capitals of the world within the space of twenty-four hours."

As soon as Napoleon was crowned Emperor of France, the senators of the Italian Republic, over which he had been elected president, sent an earnest petition that he would be crowned their king at Milan. Napoleon had rescued them from the hated dominion of the Austrians, and they regarded him as their greatest benefactor. The emperor was in the habit of setting out on his various tours without any warning. One evening, when the festivities of the baptism of the second son of Hortense had been kept up until midnight, Napoleon said quietly, upon retiring, "Horses at six for Italy." Josephine accompanied her husband upon this tour. The road bridging the Alps, which Napoleon subsequently constructed, was then but contemplated. It was only by a rugged and dangerous foot-path that the ascent of these awful barriers of nature could be surmounted. Two beautiful sedans had been constructed in Turin for the emperor and empress. The one for Napoleon was lined with crimson silk, richly ornamented with gold. Josephine's was trimmed with blue satin, similarly ornamented with silver. The sedans were, however, but little used, except in places where walking was dangerous, as the empress very much preferred leaning upon the arm of her husband, and, in conversation with him, gazing upon the wild sublimities with which they were surrounded. This must have been to Josephine, independently of those inward anxieties which weighed so heavily upon her heart, as delightful a journey as a mortal can enjoy. All Europe was bowing in homage before her illustrious husband. He was in the possession of power such as the proudest of the Cæsars might have envied. Illuminations, and triumphal arches, and enthusiastic acclamations met them every step of their way. Josephine was in the possession of every possible acquisition earth could give to make her happy, save only one—her husband was not a father. But Josephine forgot her solicitudes in the exultant hours when her husband, from the pinnacles of the Alps, pointed out to her the glories of sunny Italy—the scenes of past perils, and conflict, and renown—the fields in which he had led the armies of France to the most brilliant victories. Napoleon was in fine spirits, and in these gilded hours he looked lovingly upon her, and they both were truly happy. It is difficult for the imagination to conceive any thing more attractive for a warm-hearted and an enthusiastic woman than to pass over these most sublime of the barriers of nature, with Napoleon for a guide and a confiding friend. Pope Pius VII., who had formed a very strong friendship for Josephine, accompanied them as far as Turin. When parting, the empress made him a present of a beautiful vase of Sèvres china, embellished with exquisite paintings of the coronation.

From Turin Napoleon took Josephine to the field of Marengo. He had assembled upon that great battle plain, which his victory has immortalized, thirty thousand troops, that Josephine might behold, in the mimicry of war, the dreadful scenes which had deluged those fields in blood. It was the fifth of May, and a bright Italian sun shone down upon the magnificent pageant. A vast elevation was constructed in the middle of the plain, from which, seated upon a lofty throne, the emperor and empress overlooked the whole field. Napoleon decorated himself upon the occasion with the same war-worn garments—the battered hat, the tempest-torn cloak, the coat of faded blue, and the long cavalry saber which he had worn amid the carnage and the terror of that awful day. Many of the veterans who had been engaged in the action were present. Napoleon and Josephine came upon the ground in a magnificent chariot, drawn by eight horses. The moment he appeared upon the plain, one general shout of acclamation from thirty thousand adoring voices rent the sky. After the mimic battle was ended, the soldiers defiled before the emperor and empress, while he conferred, upon those who had signalized themselves in the day of Marengo, the decorations of the Legion of Honor. The gorgeous uniform of the men, the rich caparisons and proud bearing of the horses, the clangor of innumerable trumpets and martial bands, the glitter of gold and steel, the deafening thunders of artillery and musketry, filling the air with one incessant and terrific war; the dense volumes of sulphurous smoke rolling heavily over the plain, shutting out the rays of an unclouded sun, all combined to produce an effect upon the spectators never to be effaced.

On the eighth of May, 1805, they made their triumphal entry into the city of Milan. While the whole city was absorbed in those fêtes and rejoicings which preceded the coronation, the inexhaustible mind of Napoleon was occupied in planning those splendid public buildings and those magnificent improvements which still commemorate the almost superhuman energy of his reign. The iron crown of Charlemagne, which for a thousand years had pressed no brow, was brought forth from its mausoleum to add the attraction of deep poetic sentiment to the coronation. The ceremony took place on the twenty-sixth of May, in the Cathedral of Milan. The coronation was conducted with magnificence not even surpassed by the ceremony in Nôtre Dame. The empress first made her appearance, most gorgeously dressed, and glittering with diamonds. She was personally loved by the Milanese, and was greeted with the most enthusiastic acclamations. A moment after, the emperor himself entered, by another door. He was arrayed in imperial robes of velvet, purple, and gold, with the diadem upon his brow, and the iron crown and scepter of Charlemagne in his hands. Napoleon, as in the coronation at Paris, refused to receive the crown from the hands of another, but placed it himself upon his head, repeating aloud the historical words, "God has given it to me; woe to him who touches it." Josephine then knelt upon an altar at his feet, and was again crowned by her husband.

Josephine remained with the emperor in Milan for nearly a month. He was busy night and day in commencing improvements of the most majestic character. The Italians still look back to the reign of Napoleon as the brightest period in their history. The gay Milanese surrendered themselves, during his stay, to one continued scene of festivity. One day Josephine and Napoleon had broken away from courtiers and palaces, and all the pageantry of state, and had retreated for a few hours to the retirement and solitude of a beautiful little island in one of the lakes in that vicinity. They entered the cabin of a poor woman. She had no idea of the illustrious character of her guests, and, in answer to their kind inquiries, opened to them the story of her penury, her toils, and her anxiety to bring up her three children, as the father often could obtain no work. "Now how much money, my good woman," inquired Napoleon, "would you like to have to make you perfectly happy?" "Ah! sir," she replied, "a great deal of money I should want." "But how much should you desire if you could have your wish." "Oh, sir, I should want as much as twenty louis (about eighty dollars); but what prospect is there of our ever having twenty louis?" The emperor poured into her lap three thousand francs (about six hundred dollars) in glittering gold. For a few moments she was speechless in bewilderment; at length, trembling with emotion, she said, "Ah! sir—ah! madam, this is a great deal too much. And yet you do not look as if you could sport with the feelings of a poor woman." "No!" Josephine replied, in the most gentle accents. "The money is all yours. With it you can now rent a piece of ground, purchase a flock of goats, and I hope you will be able to bring up your children comfortably."

From Milan the emperor and empress continued their tour to Genoa. The restless mind of Napoleon was weary even of the swiftest speed of the horses, and though they drove from post to post with the utmost possible rapidity, so that it was necessary continually to throw water upon the glowing axle, he kept calling from his carriage, "On! on! we do not go fast enough." Their reception at Genoa was unequaled by any thing they had before witnessed. In the beautiful bay a floating garden of orange-trees and rare plants and shrubbery was constructed in honor of Josephine. In the principal church of "Genoa the Superb," the emperor and empress received the allegiance of the most prominent inhabitants. The fêtes on this occasion almost surpassed the creations of fancy. The senses were bewildered by the fairy illusions thrown around the gorgeous spectacle. The city, with all its picturesque beauty of embattled forts and craggy shores—the serenity and brilliance of Italian skies in May—the blue expanse of the Mediterranean—the marble palaces and glittering domes which embellished the streets—the lovely bay whitened with sails—all combined to invest the gorgeous spectacle with attractions such as are rarely witnessed. From Genoa they proceeded to Paris, every where accompanied by the thunders of artillery and the blaze of illuminations.

Josephine was not unfrequently under the necessity of taking journeys unaccompanied by the emperor. On such occasions the tireless mind of Napoleon arranged every particular with the utmost precision.

A manuscript was placed in her hand, describing the route she was to take, the places at which she was to stop, the addresses or replies she was to make to public functionaries, the expenses she was to incur, and even the presents she was to make. On such excursions, Josephine every morning most carefully studied her lesson for the day. She took great pleasure in obeying his directions exactly, exposing herself to great inconveniences rather than to allow herself to deviate in the slightest particular from the written directions. She was ever unwilling to listen to any suggestions for change. A very interesting illustration of her scrupulous adherence to manuscript instructions occurred in her journey to Liege.

Napoleon, in the directions given to Josephine, had marked out her route by a road through the forest of Ardennes. Napoleon had ordered that road to be constructed, and supposed that it was completed. It was, however, only partially made, and it was considered quite unsafe to attempt to pass over it with carriages. She inquired if it were possible to pass. Being told that it was *possible*, perhaps, but that the attempt would be attended with great difficulty and danger, she replied, "Very well, then; we will at least try." Some of the ladies accompanying her entreated her to take another route. "No," she replied; "Napoleon has requested me to take this road, and his wishes are my law." Josephine persevered in the attempt, and accomplished the passage through, though with very great difficulty. In many places the workmen on the road had to support the carriages with ropes and poles to prevent an overturn. It rained during much of the journey. Josephine and her ladies were often compelled to alight, and to walk for some distance nearly ankle deep in mud and water. Josephine endured all with the utmost good nature. She was cheered by the assurance that she was following the wishes of her husband. Many of her attendants, however, were excessively annoyed by the hardships they encountered. The carriage of the first femme-de-chambre was actually overturned, and the irritated serving-woman could not restrain her expressions of impatience and displeasure. At last one of the distinguished ladies of the court took it upon herself to lecture the empress so roundly for her blind subservience to the directions of Napoleon, that Josephine burst into tears.

Josephine, by conversation, observation, and reading, was continually storing her mind with valuable information. In the various journeys she took, she was always accompanied by persons of intelligence, and who were well acquainted with the country. While traveling, she directed her conversation almost exclusively upon the scenes through which they were passing. Every thing of interest was carefully treasured up in her memory, and if she learned any incident connected with the past fortunes of any of the families of the ladies who were with her, she never failed to send a special messenger with the information, and to point out the places where such incidents occurred. She seemed thus to be continually studying for opportunities of manifesting kind and delicate attentions to the ladies of her household. She thus secured a universality and a fervor of affection such as has rarely been attained. On these pleasure excursions, the restraints of the court were laid aside, and there were all the joyous commingling and affectionate familiarity which prevail among intimate friends.

Napoleon, aware of the vast influence which the pomp of regal state exerts upon the human mind, was very particular in his court in the observance of all the etiquette of royalty. Josephine, however, was always disposed to escape from the exactions of the code ceremonial whenever she could do so with propriety. A curious instance of this occurred at Aix la Chapelle, where the empress was passing a few days for the benefit of the baths. One evening she was sitting, with her ladies around her, weary of the lassitude of a fashionable watering-place, when some one suggested that, to while away an hour, they should visit a celebrated model of Paris, which was then on exhibition. The chevalier of honor was about to order the imperial carriages and the cortège, when Josephine, to his utter consternation, proposed that they should go on foot. She was sure, she said, that the citizens of Aix la Chapelle were so kindly disposed toward her, that there could be no possible danger. The chevalier, as far as he dared to do, urged his remonstrances against such a breach of imperial decorum; but the ladies of the court were all delighted with the plan of Josephine, and they set out on foot, a brilliant party of ladies and gentlemen, to visit the exhibition. As the citizens, of course, knew nothing about this unexpected movement, there was no crowd in the streets to impede their way, and they proceeded without any difficulty, and very pleasantly, to the place of their destination. But the intelligence of the adventure of the court, so novel and so unprecedented, was immediately noised throughout the town. From every section of the city, throngs, allured by curiosity and love for Josephine, began to pour into the streets through which they were to pass to see them return. The citizens occupying the dwellings and the shops which lined the streets, instantly, and as if by magic, illuminated their windows. A thousand hands were busy in the eager and love-incited toil. The party spent an hour examining the beautiful model of the metropolis, and then emerged again into the street. To their surprise, and not a little to their consternation, they found their path blazing with illuminations. Their whole route was filled with a dense throng of men, women, and children, all eager to catch a glimpse of their beloved empress, and of the brilliant suite which accompanied her.

The ladies recoiled from attempting the passage on foot through such a crowd, and proposed sending for the carriages and escort. Josephine, apprehensive that some accident might occur in attempting to drive the horses through such a dense mass of people, would not listen to the suggestion. "Were any one to be injured," she said, "of these friends whom our imprudence has assembled, I never could forgive myself." Taking the arm of the chevalier, she led the way through the crowd. The ladies all followed, each supported by the arm of some nobleman of the court. The populace respectfully opened before them, and closed up behind. The plumes, and diamonds, and gay attire of the court shone brilliantly in the blaze of light which was shed upon them from the illuminated windows. The enthusiastic acclamations of the populace greeted the empress until she arrived, in perfect safety, at her residence. As soon as she entered her saloon, with her accustomed frankness she thanked the chevalier for the advice which he had given, and confessed that, in not following it, she had been guilty of imprudence, which might have been attended by very serious consequences.

When traveling unaccompanied by the emperor, she was fond of breakfasting in the open air, upon some green lawn, beneath the shade of venerable trees, or upon some eminence, where her eye could feast upon the sublimities of Nature, which are so attractive to every ennobled mind. The peasantry, from a respectful distance, would look upon the dazzling spectacle perfectly bewildered and awe-stricken. The service of silver and of gold, the luxurious viands, the gorgeous display of graceful female attire, and uniforms and liveries, all combined to invest the scene, in their eyes, with a splendor almost more than earthly.

On one occasion, a mother's love and pride triumphed over even her scrupulous obedience to the wishes of Napoleon. Napoleon and Josephine, accompanied by Eugene and a very magnificent retinue, were at Mayence. There was to be a grand presentation of the German princes to the emperor and empress. Eugene, the son of the empress, according to the laws of court etiquette, should have been included with Napoleon and Josephine in the presentation. By some oversight, his name was omitted. As Josephine glanced her eye over the programme, she noticed the omission, and pointed it out to Napoleon. As the arrangements had all been made by him, he was not a little piqued in finding himself at fault as to a point of etiquette, and insisted upon following the programme. Josephine, ever ready to make any personal sacrifice to meet the wishes of Napoleon, could not be induced to sacrifice the sensitive feelings of her son. "I had no desire," she said, "for the honors of coronation; but, since I have been crowned, my son must be treated as the son of an empress." Napoleon yielded, not, however, with very good grace.

Two of the princesses of Baden, on this occasion, accompanied Josephine to the opera. The evening air was chilly, and the empress, observing that they were very thinly clad, spread over the shoulders of each of them one of her rich white Cashmere shawls. These shawls were of the most costly texture, and had been purchased at an expense of several thousand dollars. The next morning the elder of the princesses sent a note, full of complimentary terms, to Josephine, expressing their infinite obligation for her kindness, and stating that they would keep the shawls in remembrance of one they so greatly admired.

On these journeys Napoleon was full of pleasantry, and very agreeable. Josephine often spoke of this excursion to Mayence in particular as the most delightful that she had ever made with the emperor. They were met at every step on their route with the most enthusiastic testimonials of a nation's love and gratitude. And Napoleon had at this time conferred benefits upon France which richly entitled him to all this homage. In subsequent years, when intoxicated by the almost boundless empire he had obtained, and when, at a still later period, he was struggling, with the energies of despair, against Europe, in arms to crush him, he resorted to acts which very considerably impaired his good name. Josephine, in her journal during this journey, speaks of the common, but erroneous impression, that Napoleon could work constantly and habitually with very few hours devoted to sleep. She says that this was an erroneous impression. If the emperor rose at a very early hour in the morning, he would frequently retire at nine o'clock in the evening. And when, on extraordinary occasions, he passed many nights together in almost sleepless activity, he had the faculty of catching short naps at intervals in his carriage, and even on horseback. After many days and nights of preparation for some great conflict, he has been known even to fall asleep upon the field of battle, in the midst of all the horrors of the sanguinary scene. At the battle of Bautzen, for instance, Napoleon was extremely fatigued by the exertions and sleeplessness of the two preceding days and nights. He fell asleep several times when seated on an eminence, overlooking the field of battle, and which was frequently reached by the cannon balls of the enemy. Napoleon, at St. Helena, when alluding to this fact, said that Nature had her rights, which could not be violated with impunity; and that he felt better prepared to issue fresh orders, or to consider the reports which were brought, when awaking from these momentary slumbers. Though Napoleon could not set at defiance the established workings of our mental and physical nature, words can hardly convey an adequate idea of the indefatigable activity of his mind, or of his extraordinary powers of enduring mental and bodily fatigue. Few have ever understood better the art of concentrating the attention upon one thing at a time. Often, on his campaigns, after reading the dispatches, and dictating orders to one set of secretaries during the whole day, he would throw himself, for an hour, upon his sofa, instantly fall into the soundest sleep, and then, summoning to his presence a new relay of secretaries, would keep them incessantly occupied till morning. To keep himself awake on such occasions, he resorted to strong coffee. It was only under the pressure of great necessity that he thus overtasked his Herculean powers.

Occasionally, when Napoleon was absent on his campaigns, Josephine would retire to Malmaison, and become deeply interested in rural occupations. She had a large and very fine flock of merino sheep, and she took great pleasure in superintending their culture. A detachment of the imperial guard was, on such occasions, appointed to do duty at Malmaison. One evening the empress, sitting up till a later hour than usual, heard the sound of footsteps passing to and fro beneath her window. She sent for the officer of the guard, and inquired what it meant. He informed her that it was the sentry, who was appointed to keep watch beneath her window all night. "Sir," she replied, "I have no need of a night-guard. These brave soldiers have enough to suffer from the hardships of war when they are under the necessity of going to the field of battle. In my service they must have repose. I wish them here to have no sleepless nights."

It is said that rather a ludicrous occurrence took place in one of the cities of the Rhine, in reference to a visit which the emperor and empress were about to make to that place. One of the distinguished ladies of the city, who was anticipating the honor of a presentation, wrote to obtain from the master of the ceremonies instructions respecting the etiquette to be observed. The answer contained very minute directions, and was couched in terms which conveyed a deep impression of their importance. Among other things, it was stated that three courtesies were to be made; one immediately upon entering the saloon, one in the middle of the room, and a third, *en pirouette*, when having arrived within a few paces of the emperor and empress. The familiar signification of *en pirouette* is whirling the body around rapidly upon the toes of one foot, the other foot being rather indecorously raised. The ladies assembled to study these instructions; and though some of the young, the beautiful, and the graceful were not unwilling thus to display their lightness of limb, there were others who read *en pirouette* with consternation. The vast importance which Napoleon attached to every form of etiquette was well known. There was no alternative; the fat and the lean, the tall and the short, the graceful and the awkward, all were to approach their majesties *en pirouette*, or to lose the honor of a presentation. "We have a fortnight for practice," said one of the ladies; "let us prepare ourselves." For fifteen days all the drawing-rooms of Cologne seemed to be filled with dancing dervishes. Venerable dowagers were twirling like opera girls, and not unfrequently measuring their portly length upon the carpet. *En pirouette* was the theme of every tongue, and the scene, morning, noon, and evening, in every ambitious saloon.

On the evening of the arrival of the emperor and empress, the same lady who had written the letter for instructions called upon one of the ladies of the court for still more precise directions. She then learned that, in court phrase, *en pirouette* simply indicated a slight inclination of the body toward their majesties, accompanying the courtesy. The intelligence was immediately disseminated through Cologne, to the great relief of some, and, probably, not a little to the disappointment of others. Josephine was exceedingly amused at the recital of this misunderstanding.

Josephine was often accused of extravagance. Her expenditures were undoubtedly very great. She attached no value to money but as a means of promoting happiness. She was, perhaps, too easily persuaded to purchase of those who were ever urging upon her the most costly articles, and appealing powerfully to her sympathies to induce her to buy. It was difficult for Josephine to turn a deaf ear to a tale of distress. Napoleon was ever ready to spend millions upon millions in great public improvements, but he was not willing to have any money wasted. Josephine gave away most liberally in charity, and the emperor, at times, complained a little of the large sums which escaped through her hands. In replying once to a friend, who told her that she was deemed extravagant, she said, "When I have money, you know how I employ it. I give it principally to the unfortunate, who solicit my assistance, and to the poor emigrants. But I will try to be more economical in future. Tell the emperor so if you see him again. But is it not my duty to bestow as much charity as I can?"

On one occasion Napoleon was much displeased by hearing that Josephine had suffered General Lorges, the commandant at Aix la Chapelle, a young and handsome man, to be guilty of the indiscretion of sitting upon the same sofa with the empress. He reproached her with much severity for permitting such indecorum. Josephine explained the circumstances. Instead of its being General Lorges who had thus violated the rules of courtly propriety, it was one of the aged and veteran generals of Napoleon's army, who, inured to the hardships of the camp, was entirely unacquainted with the politeness of courts. He had been presented to Josephine, and, without any consciousness of the impropriety of which he was guilty, immediately seated himself upon the same sofa with the empress. Josephine was unwilling to wound the feelings of the honest-hearted old soldier, and permitted him to retain his seat until he withdrew. Napoleon was perfectly satisfied with the explanation, and, upon receiving it, manifested renewed indications of the affection and esteem with which he regarded the empress.

About this time Josephine was informed of the contemplated alliance between Eugene and the Princess-royal of Bavaria. She was soon summoned to Munich to attend their nuptials, and there again was united to those she so dearly loved. The bride of Eugene was in every respect worthy of him, and Josephine rejoiced over the happiness of her son. The victorious emperor and empress then returned to Paris, accompanied by a crowd of princes from the various courts of Germany. Josephine was now upon the very summit of earthly grandeur. Europe lay prostrate at the feet of her husband. Hortense was Queen of Holland. Eugene was Viceroy of Italy, and son-in-law to the King of Bavaria. Napoleon, fixing his affections upon the eldest child of Hortense, appeared to have relinquished the plan of the divorce, and to have contemplated the recognition of this child—the brother of Louis Napoleon, now President of the French Republic—as the heir of his crown. The embarrassment which had at times accompanied their interviews had consequently passed away. Napoleon was proud of Josephine, and often said that there was no woman in the world to be compared with her. The empress was happy. All France was filled with stories of her active benevolence and her sympathy with the sorrowful. Wherever she made her appearance, she was greeted with the acclamations of the most enthusiastic attachment.

Of the many tours which Josephine took with Napoleon, she frequently kept a journal, noting down the events of interest which occurred. The fragments of these journals, which have appeared before the public, beautifully exhibit the literary taste and the benevolence of heart of the empress. The following is an extract:

> "About two leagues from Bayonne the emperor was presented with a spectacle worthy of him. On the declivity of a mountain, gently scooped out in different parts of its descent, is pitched one of those camps which the foresight of the country has provided for its defenders. It is composed of seven handsome barracks, different in form and aspect, each isolated, surrounded with an orchard in full bearing, a well-stocked poultry-yard, and, at different distances, a greater or less quantity of arable land, where a diversity of soil yields a variety of produce. One side of the mountain is wild, but picturesque, with rocks and plants. The other seems covered with rich tapestry, so varied and numerous are the

plots of highly-cultivated ground. The summit is clothed with an ever-verdant forest. Down the center, in a deep channel, flows a limpid stream, refreshing and fertilizing the whole scene. On this spot, the veterans who occupy it gave a fête to the emperor which was at once military and rural. The wives, daughters, and little children of these brave men formed the most pleasing, as they were themselves the noblest ornament of the festival. Amid piles of arms were seen beautiful shrubs covered with flowers, while the echoes of the mountain resounded to the bleating of flocks and the warlike strains of a soldiery intoxicated on thus receiving their chief. The emperor raised this enthusiasm to the highest pitch by sitting down at a table at once quite military and perfectly pastoral. I dare not mention the attentions of which I was the object. They affected me deeply. I regarded them as proofs of that veneration which France has vowed to the emperor."

The infamous Ferdinand of Spain, who was then claiming the throne, in a disgraceful quarrel with his equally infamous father, sent an embassador to Bayonne to meet the emperor. Ferdinand, with the utmost servility, was courting the support of Napoleon. The embassador possessed, some leagues from Bayonne, an extensive farm, on which were bred numerous flocks of merinoes. "Thither," writes Josephine, "under a plausible pretext, we were conducted to-day. After a feast of really rustic magnificence, we made the tour of the possession on foot. At the bottom of a verdant dell, surrounded on all sides by rocks, covered with moss and flowers, all of a sudden a picturesque cot appeared, lightly suspended on a projecting point of rock. Around it were feeding seven or eight hundred sheep of the most beautiful breed. We could not restrain a cry of admiration. Upon the emperor addressing some compliments to the embassador, he declared that these flocks belonged to me. 'The king, my master,' he added, 'knows the empress's taste for rural occupations, and as this species of sheep is little known in France, and will constitute the principal ornament, and, consequently, wealth of a farm, he entreats her not to deprive herself of an offering at once so useful and so agreeable.' 'Don Pedro,' replied the emperor, with a tone of severity, 'the empress can not accept a present save from the hand of a king, and your master is not yet one. Wait, before making your offering, till your own nation and I have decided.'"

The ordinary routine of life with her, as empress, was as follows. Constant, the valet de chambre of Napoleon, gives the following account of the commencement of the day. "I had a regular order to enter the emperor's apartment at seven o'clock. When the empress passed the night there, it was a very unusual occurrence not to find the august spouses awake. The emperor commonly asked for tea or an infusion of orange-flowers, and rose immediately after. In the course of a few minutes the empress rose also, and, putting on a loose morning-gown, either read the journals while the emperor dressed, or retired by a private access to her own apartments, but never without addressing some kind and condescending words to myself."

Josephine invariably commenced her morning toilet at nine o'clock. This occupied an hour, and then she passed into a saloon where she received those who had obtained the favor of a morning presentation. A great many petitions were presented her on such occasions, and, with unvarying kindness, she manifested great firmness in rejecting those which appeared unworthy of her support. These audiences occupied an hour, and then she met, at eleven o'clock, the most distinguished ladies of the court at the breakfast-table. Napoleon, entirely engrossed by those majestic plans he was ever conceiving and executing, usually breakfasted alone in his cabinet, very hastily, not allowing more than seven or eight minutes to be occupied by the meal. After breakfast, Josephine, with her ladies, took a short walk, if the weather was fair, or for half an hour played a game of billiards. The remainder of the morning, until three o'clock, she passed in her apartment, with her chosen female friends, reading, conversing, and embroidering. Josephine herself was an admirable reader, and the book they were perusing was passed alternately from hand to hand. No works were read but those of real value. By common consent, all novels were banished from the circle, as Napoleon inveterately abominated every work of that kind. If he happened to find a novel in the hands of any of the attendants of the palace, he unhesitatingly tossed it into the fire, and roundly lectured the reader upon her waste of time. If Josephine had been a novel reader, she never could have acquired that mental energy which enabled her to fill with dignity and with honor every position she was called to occupy.

Occasionally Napoleon would leave his cabinet and enter the apartment of the empress where the ladies were reading. His presence was ever cordially greeted, and, with great sociability, he would for a few moments converse with his friends, and then return to his work. Not unfrequently the emperor wished to confer with Josephine upon some subject of moment. A gentle tap from his hand at the door of private communication announced to the empress the summons, which she ever most joyfully obeyed. Occasionally these interviews were protracted for several hours, for the emperor had learned to repose great confidence in many matters upon the sound judgment of Josephine.

At three o'clock the carriages were at the door, and Josephine, with her ladies, rode out. It was very seldom that Napoleon could find time to accompany them. On returning from the drive, she dressed for dinner. Napoleon attached much importance to this grand toilet, for he was fully aware of the influence of costume upon the public mind, and was very fond of seeing Josephine dressed with elegance and taste. It is reported that he not unfrequently recreated himself by entering her boudoir on such occasions, and suggesting the robe or the jewelry he would like to have her wear. Her waiting-women were not a little embarrassed by the manner in which his unskillful hands would throw about the precious contents of the caskets, and the confusion into which he would toss all the nameless articles of a lady's wardrobe.

Dinner was appointed at six o'clock. It was, however, served when Napoleon was ready to receive it. Not unfrequently, when much engrossed with business, he would postpone the hour until nine, and even ten o'clock. The cook, during all this time, would be preparing fresh viands, that a hot dinner might be ready at a moment's warning. A chicken, for instance, was put upon the spit every fifteen minutes. Napoleon and Josephine always dined together, sometimes alone, more frequently with a few invited guests. There was a grand master of ceremonies, who, on all such occasions, informed the grand marshal of the necessary arrangements, and of the seat each guest was to occupy.

Occasionally the emperor and empress dined in state. Rich drapery canopied the table, which was placed upon a platform, slightly elevated, with two arm-chairs of gorgeous workmanship, one for Napoleon, and the other, upon his left, for Josephine. Other tables were placed upon the floor of the same room for illustrious guests. The grand marshal announced to the emperor when the preparations for them to enter the room was completed. A gorgeous procession of pages, marshals, equeries, and chamberlains accompanied the emperor and empress into the hall. Pages and stewards performed the subordinate parts of the service at the table, in bringing and removing dishes, while noblemen of the highest rank felt honored in ministering to the immediate wants of their majesties. Those who sat at the surrounding tables were served by servants in livery.

Josephine passed the evening in her apartment almost invariably with a party either of invited guests, or of distinguished ministers and officers of the empire, who, having called on business, were awaiting the pleasure of Napoleon. There were frequent receptions and levees, which filled the saloons of the palace with a brilliant throng. At midnight all company retired, and the palace was still. Josephine loved the silence of these midnight hours, when the turmoil of the day had passed, and no sounds fell upon her ear but the footfalls of the sentinel in the courtyard below. She often sat for an hour alone, surrendering herself to the luxury of solitude and of undisturbed thought.

Such was the general routine of the life of Josephine while empress. She passed from one to another of the various royal residences, equally at home in all. At the Tuilleries, St. Cloud, Versailles, Rambouillet, and Fontainebleau, life was essentially the same. Occasionally, at the rural

THE HISTORY OF JOSEPHINE

palaces, hunting parties were formed for the entertainment of distinguished guests from abroad. Napoleon himself took but little personal interest in sports of this kind. On such occasions, the empress, with her ladies, usually rode in an open calêche, and a pic-nic was provided, to be spread on the green turf, beneath the boughs of the forest. Once a terrified, panting stag, exhausted with the long chase, when the hounds in full bay were just ready to spring upon him, by a strange instinct sought a retreat beneath the carriage in which the gentle heart of Josephine was throbbing. The appeal was not in vain. Josephine plead for the life of the meek-eyed, trembling suppliant. To mark it as her favorite, and as living under the shield of her protection, she had a silver collar put around its neck. The stag now roamed its native glades unharmed. No dog was permitted to molest it, and no sportsman would injure a protégé of Josephine. Her love was its talisman.

The following letter, which at this time she wrote to Caroline, the sister of Napoleon, who had married Murat, will show the principles, in the exercise of which Josephine won to herself the love of all hearts.

> "Our glory, the glory of woman, lies in submission; and if it be permitted us to reign, our empire rests on gentleness and goodness. Your husband, already so great in the opinion of the world through his valor and exploits, feels as if he beheld all his laurels brought to the dust on appearing in your presence. You take a pride in humbling him before your pretensions; and the title of being the sister of a hero is, with you, reason for believing yourself a heroine. Believe me, my sister, *that* character, with the qualities which it supposes, becomes us not. Let us rejoice moderately in the glory of our husbands, and find our glory in softening their manners, and leading the world to pardon their deeds. Let us merit this praise, that the nation, while it applauds the bravery of our husbands, may also commend the gentleness bestowed by Providence on their wives to temper their bravery."

The palace ever seemed desolate when Napoleon was absent, and Josephine was always solicitous to accompany him upon his tours. Napoleon loved to gratify this wish, for he prized most highly the companionship of his only confidential friend. Upon one occasion, when he had promised to take the empress with him, circumstances arose demanding special speed, and he resolved to set out secretly without her. He ordered his carriage at one o'clock in the morning—an hour in which he supposed she would be most soundly asleep. To his amazement, just as he had stepped into his carriage, Josephine, in all the dishabille of her night-dress, with some slight drapery thrown over her person, and without even stockings upon her feet, threw herself into his arms. Some noise had at the moment awoke her, she caught an intimation of what was going on, and, without a moment's thought, sprang from her bed, threw over her a cloak, rushed down stairs, and burst into the carriage. Napoleon fondly embraced her, rolled her up warmly in his own capacious traveling pelisse, gave orders for suitable attendants to follow with the wardrobe of the empress, and the horses, with lightning speed, darted from the court-yard. "I could sooner," Napoleon would jocosely say, "transport the whole artillery of a division of my grand army, than the bandboxes of Josephine's waiting-women."

The visit which Josephine made with Napoleon to Spain gave her such an insight into the Spanish character, that she looked with much alarm upon his endeavor to place one of his brothers upon the Spanish throne. "Napoleon," said she one day to her ladies, "is persuaded that he is to subjugate all the nations of the earth. He cherishes such a confidence in his *star*, that should he be abandoned to-morrow by family and allies, a wanderer, and proscribed, he would support life, convinced that he should triumph over all obstacles, and accomplish his destiny by realizing his mighty designs. Happily, we shall never have an opportunity of ascertaining whether I am right. But of this you may rest assured, Napoleon is more courageous morally than physically. I know him better than any one else does. He believes himself predestinated, and would support reverses with as much calmness as he manifests when confronting danger on the field of battle."

Little did Josephine imagine, when uttering these sentiments, that her proud husband, before whose name the world seemed to tremble, was to die in poverty and imprisonment on the most barren island of the ocean.

The astounding energy of Napoleon was conspicuously displayed about this time in his Spanish campaign. He had placed Joseph upon the throne of Spain, and had filled the Peninsula with his armies. The Spaniards had every where risen against him, and, guided by English councils, and inspired by the tremendous energy of English arms, they had driven Joseph from his capital, had massacred, by the rage of the mob, thousands of French residents who were dwelling in the Spanish cities, and were rapidly driving the French army over the Pyrenees. Napoleon had but just returned from the treaty of Tilsit when he was informed of this discouraging state of affairs.

He immediately, without a moment allowed for repose, set out for Spain. Josephine earnestly entreated permission to accompany the emperor. She assured him that she was fully aware of the difficulties, fatigue, and peril she must encounter, but that most cheerfully could she bear them all for the sake of being with him. She said that she should neither feel hunger nor cold, nor the need of repose, if she could but be by the side of her husband, and that all the privations of the camp would be happiness when shared with one who was all the world to her. Napoleon was deeply moved by this exhibition of her love, but, aware of the incessant activity with which it would be necessary for him to drive by night and by day, he firmly but kindly denied her request. Josephine wept bitterly as they parted.

One morning, early in November, 1808, the glittering cavalcade of the emperor, at the full gallop, drove into the encampment of the retreating French at Vittoria. The arrival of an angel, commissioned from heaven to their aid, could not have inspired the soldiers with more enthusiasm. The heavens rang with the shouts of the mighty host, as they greeted their monarch with cries of "Vive l'Empereur!" Not one moment was lost. Napoleon placed himself at the head of his concentrated army, and turning them, now inspired with the utmost confidence, against the foes before whom they had been retreating, with the resistlessness of an avalanche overwhelmed the Spanish forces. Wherever he appeared, resistance melted away before him. In the pride of achievements almost miraculous, he marched into Madrid, and there, in the capital of Spain, re-established his fallen throne. But he tarried not there an hour for indulgence or repose. The solid columns of the English army, under Sir John Moore, were still in Spain. Napoleon urged his collected forces, with all the energy which hatred could inspire, upon his English foes, and the Britons, mangled and bleeding, were driven into their ships. The conqueror, feeling that he was indeed the man of destiny, looked for a moment complacently upon Spain, again in subjection at his feet, and then, with the speed of the whirlwind, returned to Josephine at St. Cloud, having been absent but little more than two months.

In the mean time, while Napoleon was far away with his army, upon the other side of the Pyrenees, Russia, Sweden, and Austria thought it a favorable moment to attack him in his rear. They brought no accusations against the emperor, they issued no proclamation of war, but secretly and treacherously conspired to march, with all the strength of their collected armies, upon the unsuspecting emperor. It was an alliance of the kings of Europe against Napoleon, because he sat upon the throne, not by hereditary descent, the only recognized divine right, but by the popular vote. The indignation of the emperor, and of every patriotic Frenchman, had been roused by the totally unjustifiable, but bold and honest avowal of England, that peace could only be obtained by the wresting of the crown from the brow of Napoleon, and replacing it upon the head of the rejected Bourbon.

The emperor had been at St. Cloud but a short time, when, early one spring morning, a courier came dashing into the court-yard of the palace at his utmost speed, bringing the intelligence to Napoleon that Austria had treacherously violated the treaty of peace, and, in alliance with Russia, Sweden, and England, was marching her armies to invade the territory of France. The emperor, his eye flashing with indignation, hastily proceeded to the apartment of the empress with the papers communicating the intelligence in his hand. Josephine was asleep, having but just retired. He approached her bed, and, awaking her from sound slumber, requested her to be ready in two hours to accompany him to Germany. "You have played the part of an empress," said he, playfully, "long enough. You must now become again the wife of a general. I leave immediately. Will you accompany me to Strasburg?" This was short notice, but, with the utmost alacrity, she obeyed the joyful summons.

She was so accustomed to the sudden movements of the emperor that she was not often taken by surprise. Promptness was one of the most conspicuous of her manifold virtues. "I have never," she has been heard to say, "kept any one waiting for me half a minute, when to be punctual depended upon myself. Punctuality is true politeness, especially in the great."

The emperor was in glowing spirits. He had no doubt that he should be entirely victorious, and Josephine was made truly happy by that suavity and those kind attentions which he in this journey so signally displayed. Their route conducted them through some of the most beautiful and fertile valleys of France. Every where around them they saw the indications of prosperity and happiness. Napoleon was in the height of glory. The most enthusiastic acclamations of love and homage greeted the emperor and empress wherever the panting steeds which drew them rested for a moment. As they stopped for a new relay of horses in one of the little villages of Lorraine, Josephine beheld a peasant woman kneeling upon the steps of the village church, with her countenance bathed in tears. The aspect of grief ever touched the kind heart of the empress. She sent for the poor woman, and inquired into the cause of her grief.

"My poor grandson, Joseph," said she, "is included in the conscription, and, notwithstanding all my prayers, he must become a soldier. And more than this, his sister Julie was to have been married to Michael, a neighbor's son, and now he refuses to marry her because Joseph is in the conscription. And should my son purchase a substitute for poor Joseph, it would take all his money, and he would have no dowry to give Julie. And her dowry was to have been a hundred and twenty dollars."

"Take that," said the emperor, presenting the woman with a purse. "You will find enough who will be ready to supply Joseph's place for that amount. I want soldiers, and, for that purpose, must encourage marriages." Josephine was so much interested in the adventure, that, as soon as she arrived at Strasburg, she sent a valuable bridal present to Julie. The good woman's prayers were answered. From Strasburg Josephine returned to Paris, while Napoleon pressed on to encounter the combined armies of Austria and Russia in the renowned campaign of Wagram.

It was in 1805, some years before the events we have just described, that Napoleon, with his enthusiastic troops, embarked in the celebrated campaign of Ulm and Austerlitz. At Ulm he surrounded thirty thousand of his foes, and almost without a skirmish compelled them to lay down their arms. "Your master," said he to the Austrian generals, as, almost dying with mortification, they surrendered their swords, "your master wages against me an unjust war. I say it candidly, I know not for what I am fighting. I know not what he desires of me. He has wished to remind me that I was once a soldier. I trust he will find that I have not forgotten my original avocation. I will, however, give one piece of advice to my brother, the Emperor of Austria. Let him hasten to make peace. This is the moment to remember that there are limits to all empires, however powerful. The idea that the house of Lorraine may come to an end should inspire him with distrust of fortune. I want nothing on the Continent. *I desire ships, colonies, and commerce.* Their acquisition would be as advantageous to you as to me."

From Ulm, Napoleon, with two hundred thousand men, flushed with victory, rushed like a tempest down the valley of the Danube, driving the terrified Austrians before him like chaff swept by the whirlwind. Ten thousand bomb-shells were rained down upon the roofs of Vienna, till the dwellings and the streets were deluged with the blood of innocence, and then the gates were thrown open for the entrance of the conqueror. Alexander, the Emperor of all the Russias, was hastening down from the North, with his barbarian hordes, to aid the beleaguered city. Napoleon tarried not at Vienna. Fearlessly pushing on through the sleet and the hail of a Northern winter, he disappeared in the distance from the eyes of France. Austria, Sweden, Russia, were assembling their innumerable legions to crush him. He was far from home, in a hostile country. Rumors that his rashness had led to his ruin began to circulate throughout Europe.

Josephine was almost distracted with anxiety respecting her husband. She knew that a terrible battle was approaching, in which he was to encounter fearful odds. The most gloomy forebodings pervaded Paris and all France. Several days had passed, during which no intelligence whatever had been received from the distant army. Ominous whispers of defeat and ruin filled the air. The cold blasts of a December night were whistling around the towers of St. Cloud, as Josephine and a few of her friends were assembled in the saloon, anxiously awaiting tidings from Napoleon. It was no time for hilarity, and no one attempted even to promote festive enjoyment. The hour of nine o'clock had arrived, and yet no courier appeared. All hopes of any tidings on that day were relinquished. Suddenly the clatter of iron hoofs was heard as a single horseman galloped into the court-yard. Josephine almost fainted with emotion as she heard the feeble shout, "Victory—Austerlitz!" She rushed to the window and threw it open. The horse of the courier had fallen dead upon the pavement, and the exhausted rider, unable to stand, was half reclining by his side. In the intensity of her impatience, Josephine rushed down the stairs and into the court-yard, followed by all her ladies. The faithful messenger was brought to her in the arms of four men. He presented to the empress a blurred and blotted line, which the emperor had written amid the thunder and the smoke, the uproar and the carnage of the dreadful day of Austerlitz. As soon as Napoleon saw the field covered with the slain, and the routed armies of his foes flying in dismay before their triumphant pursuers, in the midst of all the horrors of that most horrible scene, he turned the energies of his impetuous mind from the hot pursuit to pen a line to his faithful Josephine, announcing the victory. The empress, with tears almost blinding her eyes, read the billet where she stood, by the light of a torch which an attendant had brought her. She immediately drew from her finger a valuable diamond ring, and presented it to the bearer of the joyful message. The messenger was Moustache the Mameluke, who had accompanied Napoleon from Egypt, and who was so celebrated for the devotion of his attachment to the emperor. He had ridden on horseback one hundred and fifty miles within twelve hours.

Napoleon was exceedingly sensitive to any apparent want of affection or attention on the part of Josephine. A remarkable occurrence, illustrative of this sensitiveness, took place on his return from his last Austrian campaign. When he arrived at Munich, where he was delayed for a short time, he dispatched a courier to Josephine, informing her that he would be at Fontainebleau on the evening of the twenty-seventh, and expressing a wish that the court should be assembled there to meet him. He, however, in his eagerness, pressed on with such unanticipated speed, that he arrived early in the morning of the twenty-sixth, thirty-six hours earlier than the time he had appointed. He had actually overtaken his courier, and entered with him the court-yard at Fontainebleau. Very unreasonably annoyed at finding no one there to receive him, he said to the exhausted courier, as he was dismounting from his horse, "You can rest to-morrow; gallop to St. Cloud, and announce my arrival to the empress." It was a distance of forty miles. Napoleon was very impatient all the day, and, in the evening, hearing a carriage enter the court-yard, he eagerly ran down, as was his invariable custom, to greet Josephine. To his great disappointment, the carriage contained only some of her ladies. "And where is the empress?" he exclaimed, in surprise. "We have preceded her by perhaps a quarter of an hour," they replied. The emperor was now in very ill humor. "A very happy arrangement," said he, sarcastically; and, turning upon his heel, he ascended to the little library, where he had been busily employed.

Soon Josephine arrived. Napoleon, hearing the carriage enter the court, coldly asked who had come. Being informed that it was the empress, he moved not from his seat, but went on very busily with his writing. The attendants were greatly surprised, for he never before had been known to omit meeting the empress at her carriage. Josephine, entirely unconscious of any fault, and delighted with the thought of again meeting her husband, and of surprising him in his cabinet, hastened up stairs and entered the room. Napoleon looked up coldly from his papers, and addressed her with the chilling salutation, "And so, madame, you have come at last! It is well. I was just about to set out for St. Cloud." Josephine burst into tears, and stood silently sobbing before him. Napoleon was conquered. His own conscience reproved him for his exceeding injustice. He rose from his seat, exclaiming, "Josephine, I am wrong; forgive me;" and, throwing his arms around her neck, embraced her most tenderly. The reconciliation was immediate and perfect, for the gentle spirit of Josephine could retain no resentment.

Napoleon had a very decided taste in reference to Josephine's style of dress, and her only ambition was to decorate her person in a manner which would be agreeable to him. On this occasion she retired very soon to dress for dinner. In about half an hour she reappeared, dressed with great elegance, in a robe of white satin, bordered with eider down, and with a wreath of blue flowers, entwined with silver ears of corn, adorning her hair. Napoleon rose to meet her, and gazed upon her with an expression of great fondness. Josephine said, with a smile, "You do not think that I have occupied too much time at my toilet?" Napoleon pointed playfully to the clock upon the mantel, which indicated the hour of half past seven, and, taking the hand of his wife, entered the dining-room.

Though Napoleon often displayed the weaknesses of our fallen nature, he at times exhibited the noblest traits of humanity. On one occasion, at Boulogne, he was informed of a young English sailor, a prisoner of war, who had escaped from his imprisonment in the interior of France, and had succeeded in reaching the coast near that town. He had secretly constructed, in an unfrequented spot, a little skiff, of the branches and bark of trees, in which fabric, almost as fragile as the ark of bulrushes, he was intending to float out upon the storm-swept channel, hoping to be picked up by some English cruiser and conveyed home. Napoleon was struck with admiration in view of the fearlessness of the project, and, sending for the young man, questioned him very minutely respecting the motives which could induce him to undertake so perilous an adventure. The emperor expressed some doubt whether he would really have ventured to encounter the dangers of the ocean in so frail a skiff. The young man entreated Napoleon to ascertain whether he was in earnest by granting him permission to carry his design into execution. "You must doubtless, then," said the emperor, "have some mistress to revisit, since you are so desirous to return to your country?" "No!" replied the sailor, "I wish to see my mother. She is aged and infirm." The heart of the emperor was touched. "You shall see her," he energetically and promptly replied. He immediately gave orders that the young man should be thoroughly furnished with all comforts, and sent in a cruiser, with a flag of truce, to the first British vessel which could be found. He also gave the young man a purse for his mother, saying, "She must be no common parent who can have trained up so affectionate and dutiful a son."

12

The Divorce and Last Days

A.D. 1807-A.D. 1814

Allusion has already been made to the strong attachment with which Napoleon cherished his little grandchild, the son of Hortense and of his brother Louis. The boy was extremely beautiful, and developed all those noble and spirited traits of character which peculiarly delighted the emperor. Napoleon had apparently determined to make the young prince his heir. This was so generally the understanding, both in France and in Holland, that Josephine was quite at ease, and serene days dawned again upon her heart.

Early in the spring of 1807, this child, upon whom such destinies were depending, then five years of age, was seized suddenly and violently with the croup, and in a few hours died. The blow fell upon the heart of Josephine with most appalling power. Deep as was her grief at the loss of the child, she was overwhelmed with uncontrollable anguish in view of those fearful consequences which she shuddered to contemplate. She knew that Napoleon loved her fondly, but she also knew the strength of his ambition, and that he would make any sacrifice of his affection, which, in his view, would subserve the interests of his power and his glory. For three days she shut herself up in her room, and was continually bathed in tears.

The sad intelligence was conveyed to Napoleon when he was far from home, in the midst of the Prussian campaign. He had been victorious, almost miraculously victorious, over his enemies. He had gained accessions of power such as, in the wildest dreams of youth, he had hardly imagined. All opposition to his sway was now apparently crushed. Napoleon had become the creator of kings, and the proudest monarchs of Europe were constrained to do his bidding. It was in an hour of exultation that the mournful tidings reached him. He sat down in silence, buried his face in his hands, and for a long time seemed lost in the most painful musings. He was heard mournfully and anxiously to repeat to himself again and again, "To whom shall I leave all this?" The struggle in his mind between his love for Josephine and his ambitious desire to found a new dynasty, and to transmit his name and fame to all posterity, was fearful. It was manifest in his pallid cheek, in his restless eye, in the loss of appetite and of sleep. But the stern will of Bonaparte was unrelenting in its purposes. With an energy which the world has never seen surpassed, he had chosen his part. It was the purpose of his soul—the purpose before which every thing had to bend—to acquire the glory of making France the most illustrious, powerful, and happy nation earth had ever seen. For this he was ready to sacrifice comfort, ease, and his sense of right. For this he was ready to sunder the strongest ties of affection.

Josephine knew Napoleon. She was fully aware of his boundless ambition. With almost insupportable anguish she wept over the death of this idolized child, and, with a trembling heart, awaited her husband's return. Mysterious hints began to fill the journals of the contemplated divorce, and of the alliance of Napoleon with various princesses of foreign courts.

In October, 1807, Napoleon returned from Vienna. He greeted Josephine with the greatest kindness, but she soon perceived that his mind was ill at ease, and that he was pondering the fearful question. He appeared sad and embarrassed. He had frequent private interviews with his ministers. A general feeling of constraint pervaded the court.

Napoleon scarcely ventured to look upon his wife, as if apprehensive that the very sight of one whom he had loved so well might cause him to waver in his firm purpose. Josephine was in a state of the most feverish solicitude, and yet was compelled to appear calm and unconstrained. As yet she had only fearful forebodings of her impending doom. She watched, with most excited apprehension, every movement of the emperor's eye, every intonation of his voice, every sentiment he uttered. Each day some new and trivial indication confirmed her fears. Her husband became more reserved, absented himself from her society, and the private access between their apartments was closed. He now seldom entered her room, and whenever he did so, he invariably knocked. And yet not one word had passed between him and Josephine upon the fearful subject. Whenever Josephine heard the sound of his approaching footsteps, the fear that he was coming with the terrible announcement of separation immediately caused such violent palpitations of the heart that it was with the utmost difficulty she could totter across the floor, even when supporting herself by leaning against the walls, and catching at the articles of furniture.

The months of October and November passed away, and, while the emperor was discussing with his cabinet the alliance into which he should enter, he had not yet summoned courage to break the subject to Josephine. The evidence is indubitable that he experienced intense anguish in view of the separation, but this did not influence his iron will to swerve from its purpose. The grandeur of his fame and the magnitude of his power were now such, that there was not a royal family in Europe which would not have felt honored in conferring upon him a bride. It was at first contemplated that he should marry some princess of the Bourbon family, and thus add to the stability of his throne by conciliating the Royalists of France. A princess of Saxony was proposed. Some weighty considerations urged an alliance with the majestic empire of Russia, and some advances were made to the court of St. Petersburgh, having in view a sister of the Emperor Alexander. It was finally decided that proposals should be made to the court of Vienna for Maria Louisa, daughter of the Emperor of Austria.

At length the fatal day arrived for the announcement to Josephine. It was the last day of November, 1809. The emperor and empress dined at Fontainebleau alone. She seems to have had a presentiment that her doom was sealed, for all that day she had been in her retired apartment, weeping bitterly. As the dinner-hour approached, she bathed her swollen eyes, and tried to regain composure. They sat down at the table in silence. Napoleon did not speak. Josephine could not trust her voice to utter a word. Neither ate a mouthful. Course after course was brought in and removed untouched. A mortal paleness revealed the anguish of each heart. Napoleon, in his embarrassment, mechanically, and apparently unconsciously, struck the edge of his glass with his knife, while lost in thought. A more melancholy meal probably was never witnessed. The attendants around the table seemed to catch the infection, and moved softly and silently in the discharge of their duties, as if they were in the chamber of the dead. At last the ceremony of dinner was over, the attendants were dismissed, and Napoleon, rising, and closing the door with his own hand, was left alone with Josephine. Another moment of most painful silence ensued, when the emperor, pale as death, and trembling in every nerve, approached the empress. He took her hand, placed it upon his heart, and in faltering accents said, "Josephine! my own good Josephine! you know how I have loved you. It is to you alone that I owe the only few moments of happiness I have known in the world. Josephine! my destiny is stronger than my will. My dearest affections must yield to the interests of France."

Josephine's brain reeled; her blood ceased to circulate; she fainted, and fell lifeless upon the floor. Napoleon, alarmed, threw open the door of the saloon, and called for help. Attendants from the ante-room immediately entered. Napoleon took a taper from the mantel, and uttering not a word, but pale and trembling, motioned to the Count de Beaumont to take the empress in his arms. She was still unconscious of every thing, but began to murmur, in tones of anguish, "Oh, no! you can not surely do it. You would not kill me." The emperor led the way, through a dark passage, to the private staircase which conducted to the apartment of the empress. The agitation of Napoleon seemed now to increase. He uttered some incoherent sentences about a violent nervous attack; and, finding the stairs too steep and narrow for the Count de Beaumont to bear the body of the helpless Josephine unassisted, he gave the light to an attendant, and, supporting her limbs himself, they reached the door of her bed-room. Napoleon then, dismissing his male attendants, and laying Josephine upon her bed, rang for her waiting-women. He hung over her with an expression of the most intense affection and anxiety until she began to revive. But the moment consciousness seemed returning, he left the room. Napoleon did not even throw himself upon his bed that night. He paced the floor until the dawn of the morning. The royal surgeon, Corvisart, passed the night at the bed-side of the empress. Every hour the restless yet unrelenting emperor called at her door to inquire concerning her situation. "On recovering from my swoon," says Josephine, "I perceived that Corvisart was in attendance, and my poor daughter, Hortense, weeping over me. No! no! I can not describe the horror of my situation during that night! Even the interest he affected to take in my sufferings seemed to me additional cruelty. Oh! how much reason had I to dread becoming an empress!"

A fortnight now passed away, during which Napoleon and Josephine saw but little of each other. During this time there occurred the anniversary of the coronation, and of the victory of Austerlitz. Paris was filled with rejoicing. The bells rang their merriest peals. The metropolis was refulgent with illuminations. In these festivities Josephine was compelled to appear. She knew that the sovereigns and princes then assembled in Paris were informed of her approaching disgrace. In all these sounds of triumph she heard but the knell of her own doom. And though a careful observer would have detected indications, in her moistened eye and her pallid cheek, of the secret woe which was consuming her heart, her habitual affability and grace never, in public, for one moment forsook her. Hortense, languid and sorrow-stricken, was with her mother.

Eugene was summoned from Italy. He hastened to Paris, and his first interview was with his mother. From her saloon he went directly to the cabinet of Napoleon, and inquired of the emperor if he had decided to obtain a divorce from the empress. Napoleon, who was very strongly attached to Eugene, made no reply, but pressed his hand as an expression that it was so. Eugene immediately dropped the hand of the emperor, and said,

"Sire, in that case, permit me to withdraw from your service."

"How!" exclaimed Napoleon, looking upon him sadly; "will you, Eugene, my adopted son, leave me?"

"Yes, sire," Eugene replied, firmly; "the son of her who is no longer empress can not remain viceroy. I will follow my mother into her retreat. She must now find her consolation in her children."

Napoleon was not without feelings. Tears filled his eyes. In a mournful voice, tremulous with emotion, he replied, "Eugene, you know the stern necessity which compels this measure, and will you forsake me? Who, then, should I have a son, the object of my desires and preserver of my interests, who would watch over the child when I am absent? If I die, who will prove to him a father? Who will bring him up? Who is to make a man of him?"

Eugene was deeply affected, and, taking Napoleon's arm, they retired and conversed a long time together. The noble Josephine, ever sacrificing her own feelings to promote the happiness of others, urged her son to remain the friend of Napoleon. "The emperor," she said, "is your benefactor—your more than father, to whom you are indebted for every thing, and to whom, therefore, you owe a boundless obedience."

The fatal day for the consummation of the divorce at length arrived. It was the 15th of December, 1809. Napoleon had assembled all the kings, princes, and princesses who were members of the imperial family, and also the most illustrious officers of the empire, in the grand saloon of the Tuilleries. Every individual present was oppressed with the melancholy grandeur of the occasion. Napoleon thus addressed them:

"The political interests of my monarchy, the wishes of my people, which have constantly guided my actions, require that I should transmit to an heir, inheriting my love for the people, the throne on which Providence has placed me. For many years I have lost all hopes of having children by my beloved spouse, the Empress Josephine. It is this consideration which induces me to sacrifice the sweetest affections of my heart, to consult only the good of my subjects, and to desire the dissolution of our marriage. Arrived at the age of forty years, I may indulge a reasonable hope of living long enough to rear, in the spirit of my own thoughts and disposition, the children with which it may please Providence to bless me. God knows what such a determination has cost my heart; but there is no sacrifice which is above my courage, when it is proved to be for the interests of France. Far from having any cause of complaint, I have nothing to say but in praise of the attachment and tenderness of my beloved wife. She has embellished fifteen years of my life, and the remembrance of them will be forever engraven on my heart. She was crowned by my hand; she shall retain always the rank and title of empress. Above all, let her never doubt my feelings, or regard me but as her best and dearest friend."

Josephine, her eyes filled with tears, with a faltering voice, replied, "I respond to all the sentiments of the emperor in consenting to the dissolution of a marriage which henceforth is an obstacle to the happiness of France, by depriving it of the blessing of being one day governed by the descendants of that great man who was evidently raised up by Providence to efface the evils of a terrible revolution, and to restore the altar, and the throne, and social order. But his marriage will in no respect change the sentiments of my heart. The emperor will ever find in me his best friend. I know what this act, commanded by policy and exalted interests, has cost his heart, but we both glory in the sacrifices we make for the good of the country. I feel elevated in giving the greatest proof of attachment and devotion that was ever given upon earth."

Such were the sentiments which were expressed in public; but in private Josephine surrendered herself to the unrestrained dominion of her anguish. No language can depict the intensity of her woe. For six months she wept so incessantly that her eyes were nearly blinded with grief. Upon the ensuing day the council were again assembled in the grand saloon, to witness the legal consummation of the divorce. The emperor entered the room dressed in the imposing robes of state, but pallid, careworn, and wretched. Low tones of voice, harmonizing with the mournful scene, filled the room. Napoleon, apart by himself, leaned against a pillar, folded his arms upon his breast, and, in perfect silence, apparently lost in gloomy thought, remained motionless as a statue. A circular table was placed in the center of the apartment, and upon this there was a writing apparatus of gold. A vacant arm-chair stood before the table. Never did a multitude gaze upon the scaffold, the block, or the guillotine with more awe than the assembled lords and ladies in this gorgeous saloon contemplated these instruments of a more dreadful execution.

At length the mournful silence was interrupted by the opening of a side door and the entrance of Josephine. The pallor of death was upon her brow, and the submission of despair nerved her into a temporary calmness. She was leaning upon the arm of Hortense, who, not possessing the fortitude of her mother, was entirely unable to control her feelings. The sympathetic daughter, immediately upon entering into the room, burst into tears, and continued sobbing most convulsively during the whole remaining scene. The assembly respectfully arose upon the entrance of Josephine, and all were moved to tears. With that grace which ever distinguished her movements, she advanced silently to the seat provided for her. Sitting down, and leaning her forehead upon her hand, she listened to the reading of the act of separation. Nothing disturbed the sepulchral silence of the scene but the convulsive sobbings of Hortense, blending with the mournful tones of the reader's voice. Eugene, in the mean time, pale and trembling as an aspen leaf, had taken a position by the side of his mother. Silent tears were trickling down the cheeks of the empress.

As soon as the reading of the act of separation was finished, Josephine for a moment pressed her handkerchief to her weeping eyes, and then, rising, in clear and musical, but tremulous tones, pronounced the oath of acceptance. She then sat down, took the pen, and affixed her signature to the deed which sundered the dearest hopes and the fondest ties which human hearts can feel. Poor Eugene could endure this anguish no longer. His brain reeled, his heart ceased to beat, and he fell lifeless upon the floor. Josephine and Hortense retired with the attendants who bore out the insensible form of the affectionate son and brother. It was a fitting termination of this mournful but sublime tragedy.

But the anguish of the day was not yet closed. Josephine, half delirious with grief, had another scene still more painful to pass through in taking a final adieu of him who had been her husband. She remained in her chamber, in heart-rending, speechless grief, until the hour arrived in which Napoleon usually retired for the night. The emperor, restless and wretched, had just placed himself in the bed from which he had ejected his most faithful and devoted wife, and the attendant was on the point of leaving the room, when the private door of his chamber was slowly opened, and Josephine tremblingly entered. Her eyes were swollen with grief, her hair disheveled, and she appeared in all the dishabille of unutterable anguish. She tottered into the middle of the room, and approached the bed; then, irresolutely stopping, she buried her face in her hands, and burst into a flood of tears. A feeling of delicacy seemed for a moment to have arrested her steps—a consciousness that she had *now* no right to enter the chamber of Napoleon; but in another moment all the pent-up love of her heart burst forth, and, forgetting every thing in the fullness of her anguish, she threw herself upon the bed, clasped Napoleon's neck in her arms, and exclaiming, "My husband! my husband!" sobbed as though her heart were breaking. The imperial spirit of Napoleon was for the moment entirely vanquished, and he also wept almost convulsively. He assured Josephine of his love

—of his ardent and undying love. In every way he tried to soothe and comfort her, and for some time they remained locked in each other's embrace. The attendant was dismissed, and for an hour they continued together in this last private interview. Josephine then, in the experience of an intensity of anguish which few hearts have ever known, parted forever from the husband whom she had so long, so fondly, and so faithfully loved.

After the empress had retired, with a desolated heart, to her chamber of unnatural widowhood, the attendant entered the apartment of Napoleon to remove the lights. He found the emperor so buried beneath the bed-clothes as to be invisible. Not a word was uttered. The lights were removed, and the unhappy monarch was left in darkness and silence to the dreadful companionship of his own thoughts. The next morning the death-like pallor of his cheek, his sunken eye, and the haggard expression of his countenance, attested that the emperor had passed the night in sleeplessness and suffering.

Great as was the wrong which Napoleon thus inflicted upon the noble Josephine, every one must be sensible of a certain kind of grandeur which pervades the tragedy. When we contemplate the brutal butcheries of Henry VIII., as wife after wife was compelled to place her head upon the block, merely to afford room for the indulgence of his vagrant passions; when we contemplate George IV., by neglect and inhumanity driving Caroline to desperation and to crime, and polluting the ear of the world with the revolting story of sin and shame; when we contemplate the Bourbons, generation after generation, rioting in voluptuousness, in utter disregard of all the laws of God and man, while we can not abate one iota of our condemnation of the great wrong which Napoleon perpetrated, we feel that it becomes the monarchies of Europe to be sparing in their condemnation.

The beautiful palace of Malmaison, which Napoleon had embellished with every possible attraction, and where the emperor and empress had passed many of their happiest hours, was assigned to Josephine for her future residence. Napoleon settled upon her a jointure of about six hundred thousand dollars a year. She was still to retain the title and the rank of Empress-Queen.

The ensuing day, at eleven o'clock, all the household of the Tuilleries were assembled upon the grand staircase and in the vestibule, to witness the departure of their beloved mistress from scenes where she had so long been the brightest ornament. Josephine descended, veiled from head to foot. Her emotions were too deep for utterance, and she waved an adieu to the affectionate and weeping friends who surrounded her. A close carriage, with six horses, was before the door. She entered it, sank back upon the cushions, buried her face in her handkerchief, and, sobbing bitterly, left the Tuilleries forever.

Josephine was still surrounded with all the external splendors of royalty. She was beloved throughout France, and admired throughout Europe. Napoleon frequently called upon her, though, from motives of delicacy, he never saw her alone. He consulted her respecting all his plans, and most assiduously cherished her friendship. It was soon manifest that the surest way of securing the favor of Napoleon was to pay marked attention to Josephine. The palace of Malmaison, consequently, became the favorite resort of all the members of the court of Napoleon. Soon after the divorce, Madame de Rochefoucault, formerly mistress of the robes to Josephine, deserting the forsaken empress, applied for the same post of honor in the household of Maria Louisa. Napoleon, when he heard of the application, promptly and indignantly replied, "She shall neither retain her old situation nor have the new one. I am accused of ungrateful conduct toward Josephine, but I do not choose to have any imitators, more especially among those whom she has honored with her confidence, and overwhelmed with benefits."

Josephine remained for some time at Malmaison. In deeds of kindness to the poor who surrounded her, in reading, and in receiving, with the utmost elegance of hospitality, the members of the court of Napoleon, who were ever crowding her saloons, she gradually regained her equanimity of spirit, and surrendered herself entirely to a quiet and pensive submission. Napoleon frequently called to see her, and, taking her arm, he would walk for hours, most confidentially unfolding to her all his plans. He seemed to desire to do every thing in his power to alleviate the intensity of anguish with which he had wrung her heart. His own affections clung still to Josephine, and her lovely and noble character commanded, increasingly, his homage. The empress was very methodical in all her arrangements, allotting to each hour its appointed duty. The description of the routine of any one day would answer about equally well for all.

Ten o'clock in the morning was the reception hour. These morning parties, attended by the most distinguished members of Parisian society, none appearing except in uniform or in court costume, were always very brilliant. Some ten or twelve of the visitors were always previously invited to remain to breakfast. At eleven o'clock they passed from the saloon to the breakfast-room, the empress leading, followed by her court according to their rank, she naming those who were to sit on her right and left. The repast, both at breakfast and dinner, ordinarily consisted of one course only, every thing excepting the dessert being placed upon the table at once. The empress had five attendants, who stood behind her chair; all the guests who sat down with her had one each. Seven officials of different ranks served at the table. The breakfast usually occupied three quarters of an hour, when the empress, with her ladies and guests, adjourned to the gallery, which contained the choicest specimens of painting and sculpture which the genius of Napoleon could select. The prospect from the gallery was very commanding, and, in entire freedom from constraint, all could find pleasant employment. Some examined with delight the varied works of art; some, in the embrasures of the windows, looked out upon the lovely scenery, and in subdued tones of voice engaged in conversation; while the chamberlain in attendance read aloud from some useful and entertaining volume to Josephine, and those who wished to listen with her. At two o'clock the arrival of the carriages at the door was the signal for the visitors to depart. Three open carriages, when the weather permitted, were always provided, each drawn by four horses. Madame d'Arberg, the lady of honor, one of the ladies in waiting, and some distinguished guest, accompanied the empress. Two hours were spent in riding, visiting improvements, and conversing freely with the various employées on the estate. The party then returned to the palace, and all disposed of their time as they pleased until six o'clock, the hour of dinner. From twelve to fifteen strangers were always invited to dine. After dinner the evening was devoted to relaxation, conversation, backgammon, and other games. The young ladies, of whom there were always many whom Josephine retained around her, usually, in the course of the evening, withdrew from the drawing-room to a smaller saloon opening from it, where, with unrestrained glee, they engaged in mirthful sports, or, animated by the music of the piano, mingled in the dance. Sometimes, in the buoyancy of youthful joy, they forgot the demands of etiquette, and somewhat incommoded, by their merry laughter, the more grave company in the grand apartment. The lady of honor would, on such occasions, hint at the necessity of repressing the mirth. Josephine would invariably interpose in their behalf. "My dear Madame d'Arberg," she would say, "suffer both them and us to enjoy, while we may, all that innocent happiness which comes from the heart, and which penetrates the heart." At eleven o'clock, tea, ices, and sweetmeats were served, and then the visitors took their leave. Josephine sat up an hour later conversing most freely and confidentially with those friends who were especially dear to her, and about midnight retired.

In the month of March, 1810, Maria Louisa arrived in Paris, and her marriage with Napoleon was celebrated with the utmost splendor at St. Cloud. All France resounded with rejoicing as Napoleon led his youthful bride into the Tuilleries, from whence, but three months before, Josephine had been so cruelly ejected. The booming of the cannon, the merry pealing of the bells, the acclamations of the populace, fell heavily upon the heart of Josephine. She tried to conceal her anguish, but her pallid cheek and swimming eye revealed the severity of her sufferings.

Napoleon continued, however, the frequency of his correspondence, and, notwithstanding the jealousy of Maria Louisa, did not at all intermit his visits. In a little more than a year after his marriage the King of Rome was born. The evening in which Josephine received the tidings of his birth, she wrote an affectionate and touching letter to Napoleon, congratulating him upon the event. This letter reveals so conspicuously the magnanimity of her principles, and yet the feminine tenderness of her bleeding heart, that we can not refrain from inserting it. It was dated at Navarre, at midnight, the 20th of March, 1811.

"Sire,—Amid the numerous felicitations which you receive from every corner of Europe, from all the cities of France, and from each regiment of your army, can the feeble voice of a woman reach your ear, and will you deign to listen to her who so often consoled your sorrows, and sweetened your pains, now that she speaks to you only of that happiness in which all your wishes are fulfilled? Having ceased to be your wife, dare I felicitate you on becoming a father? Yes, sire, without hesitation, for my soul renders justice to yours, in like manner as you know mine. I can conceive every emotion you must experience, as you divine all that I feel at this moment, and, though separated, we are united by that sympathy which survives all events.

"I should have desired to have learned the birth of the King of Rome from yourself, and not from the sound of the cannon of Evreux, or from the courier of the prefect. I know, however, that, in preference to all, your first attentions are due to the public authorities of the state, to the foreign ministers, to your family, and especially to the fortunate princess who has realized your dearest hopes. She can not be more tenderly devoted to you than I am. But she has been enabled to contribute more toward your happiness by securing that of France. She has, then, a right to your first feelings, to all your cares, and I who was but your companion in times of difficulty—I can not ask more than for a place in your affections far removed from that occupied by the empress, Maria Louisa. Not till you have ceased to watch by her bed—not till you are weary of embracing your son, will you take the pen to converse with your best friend. I will wait.

"Meanwhile, it is not possible for me to delay telling you that, more than any one in the world, do I rejoice in your joy. And you will not doubt my sincerity when I here say that, far from feeling an affliction at a sacrifice necessary for the repose of all, I congratulate myself on having made it, since I now suffer alone. But I am wrong; I do not suffer while you are happy, and I have but one regret, in not having yet done enough to prove how dear you were to me. I have no account of the health of the empress. I dare to depend upon you, sire, so far as to hope that I shall have circumstantial details of the great event which secures the perpetuity of the name you have so nobly illustrated. Eugene and Hortense will write me, imparting their own satisfaction; but it is *from you* that I desire to know if your child be well, if he resembles you, if I shall one day be permitted to see him. In short, I expect from you unlimited confidence, and upon such I have some claims, in consideration, sire, of the boundless attachment I shall cherish for you while life remains."

She had but just dispatched this letter to Napoleon, when the folding-doors were thrown open with much state, and the announcement, "From the emperor," ushered in a page, the bearer of a letter. The fragile and beautiful youth, whom Josephine immediately recognized, had so carefully secured the emperor's billet, from fear of losing it, that it took some time for him, in his slight embarrassment, to extricate it. Josephine was almost nervously excited till she received the note, and immediately retired with it to her own private apartment. Half an hour elapsed before she again made her appearance. Her whole countenance attested the intensity of the conflicting emotions with which her soul had been agitated. Her eyes were swollen with weeping, and the billet, which she still held in her hand, was blurred with her tears. She gave the page a letter to the emperor in reply, and then presented him, as an acknowledgment of her appreciation of the tidings he had brought, with a small morocco case, containing a diamond breastpin, and a thousand dollars in gold.

She then, with a tremulous voice, and smiling through her tears, read the emperor's note to her friends. The concluding words of the note were, "This infant, in concert with *our Eugene*, will constitute my happiness and that of France." As Josephine read these words with emphasis, she exclaimed, "Is it possible to be more amiable! Could any thing be better calculated to soothe whatever might be painful in my thoughts at this moment, did I not so sincerely love the emperor? This uniting of my son with his own is indeed worthy of him who, when he wills, is the most delightful of men. This is it which has so much moved me."

The emperor often afterward called upon her. He soon, notwithstanding the jealousy of Maria Louisa, arranged a plan by which he presented to Josephine, in his own arms, the idolized child. These interviews, so gratifying to Josephine, took place at the Royal Pavilion, near Paris, Napoleon and Madame Montesquieu, governess to the young prince, being the only confidants. In one of Josephine's letters to Napoleon, she says, "The moment I saw you enter, leading the young Napoleon in your hand, was unquestionably one of the happiest of my life. It effaced, for a time, the recollection of all that had preceded it, for never have I received from you a more touching mark of affection."

The apartment at Malmaison which Napoleon had formerly occupied remained exactly as it was when he last left it. Josephine herself kept the key, and dusted the room with her own hands. She would not permit a single article of furniture to be moved. The book he was last reading lay open upon the table, the map he was consulting, the pen with which he wrote, the articles of clothing which he had left in his accustomed disorder, all remained untouched. Josephine's bedchamber was very simply furnished with white muslin drapery, the only ornament being the golden toilet service which she had received from the municipality of Paris, and which, with characteristic generosity, she refused to consider as her own private property until Napoleon sent it to her. The following letter from Josephine, written at this time, pleasingly illustrates her literary polish and the refinement of her taste. It was addressed to the superintendent, ordering some alterations at Malmaison.

"Profit by my absence, dear F., and make haste to dismantel the pavilion of the acacias, and to transfer my boudoir into that of the orangery. I should wish the first apartment of the suite, and which serves for an ante-room, to be painted with light green, with a border of lilachs. In the center of the panels you will place my fine engravings from Esther, and under each of these a portrait of the distinguished generals of the Revolution. In the center of the apartment there must be a large flower-stand, constantly filled with fresh flowers in their season, and in each angle a bust of a French philosopher. I particularly mention that of Rousseau, which place between the two windows, so that the vines and foliage may play around his head. This will be a natural crown worthy of the author of Emile. As to my private cabinet, let it be colored light blue, with a border of ranunculus and polyanthus. Ten large engravings from the Gallery of the Musée, and twenty medallions, will fill up the panels. Let the casements be painted white and green, with double fillets, gilded. My piano, a green sofa, and two couches with corresponding covers, a secretaire, a small bureau, and a large toilet-glass, are articles you will not forget. In the center, place a large table, always covered with freshly-gathered flowers, and upon the mantel-shelf a simple pendule, two alabaster vases, and double-branched girandoles. Unite elegance to variety, but no profusion. Nothing is more opposed to good taste. In short, I confide to you the care of rendering this cherished spot an agreeable retreat, where I may meditate, sleep it may be, but oftenest read, which last is sufficient to remind you of three hundred volumes of my small edition."

When Josephine first retired to Malmaison, where every thing reminded her of the emperor, her grief for many months continued unabated. To divert her attention, Napoleon conferred upon her the palace of Navarre. This was formerly a royal residence, and was renowned for its magnificent park. During the Revolution it had become much dilapidated. The elegant chateau was situated in the midst of the romantic forest of Evreux. The spacious grounds were embellished by parks, whose venerable trees had withstood the storms of centuries, and by beautiful streams and crystal lakes. The emperor gave Josephine nearly three hundred thousand dollars to repair the buildings and the grounds. The taste of Josephine soon converted the scene into almost a terrestrial Eden, and Navarre, being far more retired than Malmaison, became her favorite residence.

Soon after Josephine had taken up her residence at Navarre, she wrote the following letter to Napoleon, which pleasingly illustrates the cordiality of friendship which still existed between them.

"Sire,—I received this morning the welcome note which was written on the eve of your departure for St. Cloud, and hasten to reply to its tender and affectionate contents. These, indeed, do not in themselves surprise me, but only as being received so early as fifteen days after my establishment here, so perfectly assured was I that your attachment would search out the means of consoling me under a separation necessary to the tranquillity of both. The thought that your care follows me into my retreat renders it almost agreeable.

"After having known all the rapture of a love that is shared, and all the suffering of a love that is shared no longer—after having exhausted all the pleasures that supreme power can confer, and all the happiness of beholding the man whom I loved enthusiastically admired, is there aught else, save repose, to be desired? What illusions can now remain for me? All such vanished when it became necessary to renounce you. Thus the only ties which yet bind me to life are my sentiments for you, attachment for my children, the possibility of still being able to do some good, and, above all, the assurance that you are happy. Do not, then, condole with me on my being here, distant from a court, which you appear to think I regret. Surrounded by those who are attached to me, free to follow my taste for the arts, I find myself better at Navarre than any where else, for I enjoy more completely the society of the former, and form a thousand projects which may prove useful to the latter, and which will embellish the scenes I owe to your bounty. There is much to be done here, for all around are discovered the traces of destruction. These I would efface, that there may exist no memorial of those horrible inflictions which your genius has taught the nation almost to forget. In repairing whatever these ruffians of revolution labored to annihilate, I shall diffuse comfort around me, and the benedictions of the poor will afford me infinitely more pleasure than the feigned adulation of courtiers.

"I have already told you what I think of the functionaries in this department, but have not spoken sufficiently of the respectable bishop, M. Bourlier. Every day I learn some new trait which causes me still more highly to esteem the man who unites the most enlightened benevolence with the most amiable disposition. He shall be intrusted with distributing my alms-deeds in Evreux, and, as he visits the indigent himself, I shall be assured that my charities are properly bestowed.

"I can not sufficiently thank you, sire, for the liberty you have permitted me of choosing the members of my household, all of whom contribute to the pleasure of a delightful society. One circumstance alone gives me pain, namely, the etiquette of costume, which becomes a little tiresome in the country. You fear that there may be something wanting to the rank I have preserved should a slight infraction be allowed to the toilet of these gentlemen; but I believe that you are wrong in thinking they would for one moment forget the respect due to the woman who was once your companion. Their respect for yourself, joined to the sincere attachment they bear to me, which I can not doubt, secures me from the danger of ever being obliged to recall what it is your wish that they should remember. My most honorable title is derived, not from having been crowned, but assuredly from having been chosen by you. None other is of value. That alone suffices for my immortality.

"My circle is at this time somewhat more numerous than usual, there being several visitors, besides many of the inhabitants of Evreux and the environs, whom I see of course. I am pleased with their manners, with their admiration of you, a particular in which you know that I am not easily satisfied. In short, I find myself perfectly at home in the midst of my forest, and entreat you, sire, no longer to fancy to yourself that there is no living at a distance from court. Besides you, there is nothing there which I regret, since I shall have my children with me soon, and already enjoy the society of the small number of friends who remained faithful to me. Do not forget *your friend*. Tell her sometimes that you preserve for her an attachment which constitutes the felicity of her life. Often repeat to her that you are happy, and be assured that for her the future will thus be peaceful, as the past has been stormy, and often sad."

Just before Napoleon set out on his fatal campaign to Russia, he called to see Josephine. Seated upon a circular bench in the garden, before the windows of the saloon, where they could both be seen but not overheard, they continued for two hours engaged most earnestly in conversation. Josephine was apparently endeavoring to dissuade him from the perilous enterprise. His perfect confidence, however seemed to assure her that her apprehensions were groundless. At last he arose and kissed her hand. She accompanied him to his carriage, and bade him adieu. This was their last interview but one. Soon Napoleon returned, a fugitive from Moscow. Days of disaster were darkening around his path. All Europe had risen in arms against him, and were on the march toward his capital. In the midst of the terror of those dreadful days, he sought a hurried interview with his most faithful friend. It was their last meeting. As he was taking his leave of Josephine, at the close of this short and melancholy visit, he gazed upon her a moment in silence, tenderly and sadly, and then said, "Josephine! I have been as fortunate as was ever man on the face of this earth. But, in this hour, when a storm is gathering over my head, I have not, in this wide world, any one but you upon whom I can repose."

In the fearful conflict which ensued—the most terrible which history has recorded—Napoleon's thoughts ever reverted to the wife of his youth. He kept up an almost daily correspondence with her, informing her of the passing of events. His letters, written in the midst of all the confusion of the camp, were more affectionate and confiding than ever. Adversity had softened his heart. In these dark days, when, with most Herculean power, he was struggling against fearful odds, and his throne was crumbling beneath his feet, it was observed that a letter from

Josephine was rather torn than broken open, so great was the eagerness of Napoleon to receive a line from her. Wherever he was, however great the emergency in which he was placed, the moment a courier brought to him a letter from Josephine, all other business was laid aside until it had been read.

The allied armies were every day approaching nearer and nearer to Paris, and Josephine was overwhelmed with grief in contemplating the disasters which were falling upon Napoleon. At Malmaison, Josephine and the ladies of her court were employed in forming bandages and scraping lint for the innumerable wounded who filled the hospitals. The conflicting armies approached so near to Malmaison that it became dangerous for Josephine to remain there, and, in great apprehension, she one morning, at eight o'clock, took her carriage for Navarre. Two or three times on the road she was alarmed by the cry, "Cossacks! Cossacks!" When she had proceeded about thirty miles, the pole of her carriage broke, and at the same time a troop of horsemen appeared in the distance, riding down upon her. They were French hussars; but Josephine thought that they were either Cossacks or Prussians, and, though the rain was falling in torrents, in her terror she leaped from the carriage, and began to fly across the fields. She had proceeded some distance before her attendants discovered the mistake. The carriage being repaired, she proceeded the rest of her way unmolested. The empress hardly uttered a word during this melancholy journey, but upon entering the palace she threw herself upon a couch, exclaiming, "Surely, surely Bonaparte is ignorant of what is passing within sight of the gates of Paris, or, if he knows, how cruel the thoughts which must now agitate his breast! Oh! if he had listened to me."

Josephine remained for some days at Navarre, in a state of most painful anguish respecting the fate of the emperor. She allowed herself no relaxation, excepting a solitary ride each morning in the park, and another short ride after dinner with one of her ladies. The Emperor Alexander had immediately sent a guard of honor to protect Josephine from all intrusion. Hundreds of thousands of soldiers were swarming in all directions, and every dwelling was filled with terror and distraction. One melancholy incident we will record, illustrative of hundreds which might be narrated. Lord Londonderry, in the midst of a bloody skirmish, saw a young and beautiful French lady, the wife of a colonel, in a calêche, seized by three brutal Russian soldiers, who were carrying off, into the fields, their frantic and shrieking victim. The gallant Englishman, sword in hand, rushed forward for her deliverance from his barbarian allies. He succeeded in rescuing her, and, in the confusion of the battle still raging, ordered a dragoon to take her to his own quarters till she could be provided with suitable protection. The dragoon took the lady, half dead with terror, upon his horse behind him, and was galloping with her to a place of safety, when another ruffian band of Cossacks surrounded him, pierced his body with their sabers, and seized again the unhappy victim. She was never heard of more. The Emperor Alexander was greatly distressed at her fate, and made the utmost, though unavailing efforts to discover what had become of her. The revelations of the last day alone can divulge the horrors of this awful tragedy.

The grief of Josephine in these days of anxiety was intense in the extreme. She passed her whole time in talking about Napoleon, or in reading the letters she had lately received from him. He wrote frequently, as he escaped from place to place, but many of his letters were intercepted by the bands of soldiers traversing every road. The last she had received from him was dated at Brienne. It gave an account of a desperate engagement, in which the little band of Napoleon had been overwhelmed by numbers, and was concluded with the following affecting words: "On beholding those scenes where I had passed my boyhood, and comparing my peaceful condition then with the agitation and terrors which I now experience, I several times said, in my own mind, I have sought to meet death in many conflicts; I can no longer fear it. To me death would now be a blessing. But I would once more see Josephine."

Notwithstanding the desperate state of affairs, Josephine still cherished the hope that his commanding genius would yet enable him to retrieve his fortunes. All these hopes were, however, dispelled on the receipt of the following letter:

"Fontainebleau, April 16, 1814.

"Dear Josephine,—I wrote to you on the eighth of this month, but perhaps you have not received my letter. Hostilities still continued, and possibly it may have been intercepted. At present the communications must be re-established. I have formed my resolution. I have no doubt that this billet will reach you. I will not repeat what I said to you. Then I lamented my situation, now I congratulate myself upon it. My head and spirit are freed from an enormous weight. My fall is great, but it may, as men say, prove useful. In my retreat I shall substitute the pen for the sword. The history of my reign will be curious. The world has yet seen me only in profile. I shall show myself in full. How many things have I to disclose! how many are the men of whom a false estimate is entertained! I have heaped benefits upon millions of wretches! What have they done in the end for me? They have all betrayed me—yes, all. I except from this number the good Eugene, so worthy of you and of me. Adieu! my dear Josephine. Be resigned as I am, and never forget him who never forgot, and never will forget you. Farewell, Josephine.

"Napoleon.

"P.S.—I expect to hear from you at Elba. I am not very well."

Upon reading these tidings of so terrible an overthrow, Josephine was overwhelmed with grief, and for a time wept bitterly. Soon, however, recovering her self-possession, she exclaimed, "I must not remain here. My presence is necessary to the emperor. That duty is, indeed, more Maria Louisa's than mine, but the emperor is alone—forsaken.

Well, I at least will not abandon him. I might be dispensed with while he was happy; now, I am sure that he expects me." After a pause of a few moments, in which she seemed absorbed in her own thoughts, she addressed her chamberlain, saying, "I may, however, interfere with his arrangements. You will remain here with me till intelligence be received from the allied sovereigns; they will respect her who was the wife of Napoleon."

She was, indeed, remembered by them. The magnanimity of her conduct under the deep wrongs of the divorce had filled Europe with admiration. The allied sovereigns sent her assurances of their most friendly regards. They entreated her to return to Malmaison, and provided her with an ample guard for her protection. Her court was ever crowded with the most illustrious monarchs and nobles, who sought a presentation to do homage to her virtues. The Emperor Alexander was one of the first to visit her. He said to her on that occasion, "Madam, I burned with the desire of beholding you. Since I entered France, I have never heard your name pronounced but with benedictions. In the cottage and in the palace I have collected accounts of your angelic goodness, and I do myself a pleasure in thus presenting to your majesty the universal homage of which I am the bearer."

Maria Louisa, thinking only of self, declined accompanying Napoleon to his humble retreat. Josephine, not knowing her decision, wrote to the emperor:

> "Now only can I calculate the whole extent of the misfortune of having beheld my union with you dissolved by law. Now do I indeed lament being no more than your *friend*, who can but mourn over a misfortune great as it is unexpected. Ah! sire, why can I not fly to you? Why can I not give you the assurance that exile has no terrors save for vulgar minds, and that, far from diminishing a sincere attachment, misfortune imparts to it a new force? I have been upon the point of quitting France to follow your footsteps, and to consecrate to you the remainder

of an existence which you so long embellished. A single motive restrained me, and that you may divine. If I learn that I am *the only one* who will fulfill her duty, nothing shall detain me, and I will go to the only place where, henceforth, there can be happiness for me, since I shall be able to console you when you are there isolated and unfortunate! Say but the word, and I depart. Adieu, sire; whatever I would add would still be too little. It is no longer by *words* that my sentiments for you are to be proved, and for *actions* your consent is necessary."

A few days after this letter was written, the Emperor Alexander, with a number of illustrious guests, dined with Josephine at Malmaison. In the evening twilight, the party went out upon the beautiful lawn in front of the house for recreation. Josephine, whose health had become exceedingly precarious through care and sorrow, being regardless of herself in devotion to her friends, took a violent cold. The next day she was worse. Without any very definite form of disease, she day after day grew more faint and feeble, until it was evident that her final change was near at hand. Eugene and Hortense, her most affectionate children, were with her by day and by night. They communicated to her the judgment of her physician that death was near. She heard the tidings with perfect composure, and called for a clergyman to administer to her the last rites of religion.

Just after this solemnity the Emperor Alexander entered the room. Eugene and Hortense, bathed in tears, were kneeling at their mother's side. Josephine beckoned to the emperor to approach her, and said to him and her children, "I have always desired the happiness of France. I did all in my power to contribute to it; and I can say with truth, to all of you now present, at my last moments, that the first wife of Napoleon never caused a single tear to flow."

She called for the portrait of the emperor; she gazed upon it long and tenderly; and then, fervently pressing it in her clasped hands to her bosom, faintly articulated the following prayer:

"O God! watch over Napoleon while he remains in the desert of this world. Alas! though he hath committed great faults, hath he not expiated them by great sufferings? Just God, thou hast looked into his heart, and hast seen by how ardent a desire for useful and durable improvements he was animated. Deign to approve my last petition. And may this image of my husband bear me witness that my latest wish and my latest prayer were for him and my children."

It was the 29th of May, 1814. A tranquil summer's day was fading away into a cloudless, serene, and beautiful evening. The rays of the setting sun, struggling through the foliage of the open window, shone cheerfully upon the bed where the empress was dying. The vesper songs of the birds which filled the groves of Malmaison floated sweetly upon the ear, and the gentle spirit of Josephine, lulled to repose by these sweet anthems, sank into its last sleep. Gazing upon the portrait of the emperor, she exclaimed, "L'isle d'Elbe—Napoleon!" and died.

Alexander, as he gazed upon her lifeless remains, burst into tears, and uttered the following affecting yet just tribute of respect to her memory: "She is no more; that woman whom France named the beneficent, that angel of goodness, is no more. Those who have known Josephine can never forget her. She dies regretted by her offspring, her friends, and her cotemporaries."

For four days her body remained shrouded in state for its burial. During this time more than twenty thousand of the people of France visited her beloved remains. On the 2d of June, at mid-day, the funeral procession moved from Malmaison to Ruel, where the body was deposited in a tomb of the village church. The funeral services were conducted with the greatest magnificence, as the sovereigns of the allied armies united with the French in doing honor to her memory. When all had left the church but Eugene and Hortense, they knelt beside their mother's grave, and for a long time mingled their prayers and their tears. A beautiful monument of white marble, representing the empress kneeling in her coronation robes, is erected over her burial-place, with this simple but affecting inscription:

**EUGENE AND HORTENSE
TO
JOSEPHINE.**

THE END.

ABOUT JACOB ABBOTT

Jacob Abbott was born in Hallowell, Maine in 1803, the son of a minister and farmer. Even as a young boy, he showed academic promise and an interest in spiritual matters. After attending the Hallowell Academy, he was admitted to Bowdoin College at the age of 14.

At Bowdoin, Abbott studied classics and mathematics. He graduated second in his class in 1820 at the young age of 16. He was known as a serious and studious young man who strove for excellence.

After college, Abbott went on to study at Andover Theological Seminary with the intention of becoming a Congregationalist minister. However, his rigorous study habits and frail health caused him to abandon this pursuit after just two years.

Abbott was plagued by gastrointestinal issues and migraines throughout his life, likely exacerbated by the demanding academic environment. His poor health finally forced him to leave his ministerial studies and turn to the less stressful pursuits of writing and tutoring.

First, Abbott took a job as a professor of mathematics and natural philosophy at Amherst College in 1824. The following year, he married Harriet Vaughan and moved to Boston where he opened a school for young ladies. It was during this time that he began writing simple textbooks for teaching science, history and Christian values.

So while Abbott had aspired to be a minister, chronic health issues led him to find an alternate calling educating children through clear and engaging writing. This pivot would launch his successful career as one of the most famous children's authors of the 19th century.

In 1825, Abbott married Harriet Vaughan and soon after started his own school for young ladies in Boston. During this time, he began writing educational books in a popular, simple style. His early works included the Mount Vernon Reader and The Young Christian.

Abbott gained fame with the Rollo series, first published in 1835. These stories followed a young boy named Rollo learning morals and virtues through his everyday adventures. The series was hugely popular and established Abbott's reputation as a gifted children's writer.

Other notable books by Abbott include the Franconia Stories (1853-1873), a 10-volume series about a brother and sister's adventures in the country, and the Marco Paul series (1853-1873), which followed a boy's travels around America learning about each state.

In all, Jacob Abbott wrote over 200 books, primarily for young readers. His works were praised for their ability to educate and impart moral lessons in an engaging, story-driven way. Though largely forgotten today, he was one of the most prolific and beloved children's authors of his era.

Abbott continued writing up until his death on October 31, 1879 in Farmington, Maine. His legacy lives on through his contributions to 19th century children's literature.

BIOGRAPHIES ABBOTT WROTE

A number of the books Abbott wrote were biographies of famous people. Famous characters covered in these books included:

Alexander the Great: This book provides a sweeping look at the life and achievements of Alexander III of Macedon, better known as Alexander the Great. It follows his early education by Aristotle, ascension to the throne after his father Philip II's assassination, and extensive military campaigns across Asia and northeast Africa. Abbott recounts Alexander's major battles against the Persians and annexation of their empire. The book also examines Alexander's tactics, military innovations, and creation of a Hellenistic empire stretching from Greece to India before his death at 32.

Alfred the Great: This biography focuses on Alfred's defense of the Kingdom of Wessex against Viking raids in 9th century England. It discusses how Alfred drove back the Great Heathen Army and then negotiated terms with the Vikings, designating parts of England for their settlement. Abbott also highlights Alfred's efforts to revive learning and education in England, as well as his codification of laws and strengthening of the Anglo-Saxon navy. The book frames Alfred as a scholarly, strategic and devout ruler whose achievements laid the foundation for a unified England.

King Charles I: This book looks at the reign of Charles I leading up to and during the English Civil War. It focuses on the religious and political conflicts between Charles I and Parliament, caused largely by

Charles' belief in divine right of kings and many unpopular, authoritarian policies. Abbott also examines Charles' refusal to compromise, leading to the war against Parliament's New Model Army and his eventual execution for treason in 1649 under Oliver Cromwell.

King Charles II: This biography deals with the restoration of the English monarchy under Charles II after the death of Oliver Cromwell. It follows Charles II's return from exile and re-establishment of royal power. However, Abbott also notes Charles' own conflicts with Parliament and religious controversies during his reign. The book discusses Charles' hedonistic lifestyle and many mistresses, but also his support for science, exploration and trade that helped expand the British Empire.

Cleopatra: This book examines Cleopatra VII's life and rule over ancient Egypt. Abbott chronicles Cleopatra's relationships and political alliances with Julius Caesar and Mark Antony, as she sought to maintain Egypt's independence from Rome. The biography highlights Cleopatra's intelligence, education and strategic skills in dealing with Rome. But it ultimately focuses on Cleopatra's downfall and suicide after Mark Antony's defeat by Octavian, leading to Egypt becoming a Roman province.

Cyrus the Great: This biography covers Cyrus II of Persia, founder of the Achaemenid Empire. Abbott traces Cyrus's rise from Persian prince, to revolt against the Medes, to conqueror of the Lydian and Babylonian empires. The book also examines Cyrus's leadership qualities and tolerant policies toward conquered peoples. It portrays Cyrus as a wise, inspirational leader who created the model of a centralized Persian state.

Darius: This book looks at the reign of Darius I, examining his consolidation of the Persian Empire through administrative reforms, development of infrastructure, and expansion of territory. Abbott discusses

Darius's division of the empire into provinces and implementation of a uniform tax system and coinage. The biography also covers his invasion of Greece which was thwarted at the famous Battle of Marathon. Overall, it presents Darius as an capable, pragmatic ruler under whom the Persian Empire reached its zenith.

Queen Elizabeth: This biography celebrates the long and prosperous reign of Queen Elizabeth I of England. Abbott focuses on Elizabeth's shrewd leadership, religious compromise, and patronage of the arts and literature that fostered English Renaissance culture. The book also highlights Elizabeth's naval defeat of the Spanish Armada which secured England's independence from Europe. Overall, Abbott portrays Elizabeth as a commanding, canny and popular female ruler who strengthened England as a major world power.

Genghis Khan: This book looks at the incredible rise of Temüjin, better known as Genghis Khan. It follows his hardships as an outcast youth to becoming the fearsome founder of the Mongol Empire. Abbott chronicles Genghis Khan's brilliant military tactics and utterly ruthless conquests that allowed the Mongols to dominate much of Asia and Eastern Europe. Overall it paints him as a complex figure--strategic genius but also brutal tyrant.

Hannibal: This biography focuses on the great Carthaginian general Hannibal Barca. It recounts his famous crossing of the Alps with war elephants and invasion of Italy during the Second Punic War against Rome. Abbott details Hannibal's victories in major battles like Cannae but also his eventual defeat by Scipio and exile. The book celebrates Hannibal's daring military prowess but also concession late in life that Rome could not be conquered.

Josephine: This book examines the life of Josephine Bonaparte from her aristocratic upbringing in Martinique to her marriage to Napoleon Bonaparte. It focuses on Josephine's time as Empress consort of France and her support for arts and education. But it also discusses Napoleon's eventual divorce from her due to dynastic pressures. Overall the book presents Josephine as an intelligent, compassionate woman who tempered some of Napoleon's ambition.

Julius Caesar: This traces Caesar's life from early military campaigns to dictator and eventual assassination. Abbott covers Caesar's conquest of Gaul, rivalry with Pompey, famously crossing the Rubicon and crowning as dictator. The biography also examines the conspiracy led by Brutus and Cassius to assassinate Caesar in order to save the Roman Republic. In all, the book presents Caesar as an unmatched military mind who irrevocably changed the Roman Empire.

Margaret of Anjou: This biography looks at Margaret of Anjou who became queen consort to England's King Henry VI. It focuses on the political intrigue and machinations Margaret became involved in to support her husband's reign during the War of the Roses. Abbott portrays Margaret as a fiercely devoted, cunning woman who backed the Lancastrians against factions like the Yorkists led by Richard Neville. Though she lost power, the book frames her as a dominant figure during the conflict.

Mary, Queen of Scots: This book examines the life of Mary Stuart who became Queen of Scotland as an infant. It follows her tumultuous reign marked by scandals and plots to overthrow her by Protestants. Her Catholicism also put her at odds with England's Elizabeth I. Abbott recounts Mary's forced abdication, escape to England, and eventual execution ordered by Elizabeth for plotting against her. Overall it presents a tragic figure whose life was marked by political and religious turmoil.

Nero: This biography looks at the notorious Roman emperor Nero. It explores his self-indulgent lifestyle and tyrannical rule marked by possible matricide and the brutal execution of Christians. Abbott also examines legends around Nero like his fiddling during the Great Fire of Rome. The book presents a despotic, unstable man who drastically weakened the Roman Empire.

Peter the Great: This book covers the reforms and policies of Peter the Great that rapidly westernized Russia. Abbott discusses Peter's extensive European travels as a youth and later programs to remake Russia's army, expand its naval fleet, and build a new capital in St. Petersburg. The biography also examines Peter's harsh, authoritarian approach to governing that consolidated his power. Overall it presents him as a pivotal, transformative tsar.

Pyrrhus: This examines the life and military exploits of Pyrrhus, king of Epirus. It focuses on his campaigns against Rome where he won major battles but suffered heavy losses, giving rise to the term "Pyrrhic victory." Abbott recounts Pyrrhus's struggles to build a Greek empire and failed invasion of Sicily against Carthage. Though a skilled commander, Pyrrhus ultimately failed to achieve lasting gains.

Richard I: This biography looks at the reign of Richard I, known as Lionheart. It focuses on Richard's leadership during the Third Crusade to recapture Jerusalem from Saladin. Abbott also details the legendary tales of Richard's bravery and valor in campaigns against France and during his imprisonment. Overall, the book presents Richard I as one of England's great warrior kings.

Richard II: This explores the reign and overthrow of King Richard II. Abbott covers Richard's despotic actions that led the nobles to revolt and install Henry IV, leading to Richard's imprisonment and likely murder. The biography presents a weak king whose tyranny and poor leadership during a peasant's revolt cost him power and his life.

Richard III: This delves into the controversial rule of Richard III. Abbott examines Richard's contested path to the throne and the disappearance of the Princes in the Tower which Richard likely ordered. It also portrays Richard's defeat at the hands of Henry Tudor at the Battle of Bosworth Field that ended the Wars of the Roses. Ultimately Abbott paints Richard III as willing to employ any means to gain and retain the English crown.

Romulus: This recounts the Roman legend of Romulus and Remus, twin brothers raised by a she-wolf who went on to found the city of Rome. Abbott covers the myths of the brothers' quarrel over leadership, with Romulus killing Remus and becoming Rome's first king and architect of its nascent political institutions. Though mythological, Romulus represents ancient Rome's founding origins and rise to power.

William the Conqueror: This biography follows William, Duke of Normandy's conquest of England in 1066 after victory at the Battle of Hastings. Abbott discusses William's reign as king where he consolidated control, introduced feudalism, and fused English and Norman culture. William is presented as a formidable, innovative Norman leader who irrevocably transformed Anglo-Saxon England.

Xerxes: This examines the reign of Xerxes I of Persia, known for his failed invasion of Greece. Abbott focuses on Xerxes's gathering of a massive army to crush Greek resistance, but defeat at Salamis ended his ambitions. The book covers later unrest and palace intrigue that clouded the end of Xerxes's reign. Overall he is portrayed as a rash ruler whose desire for conquest led to disaster for Persia.

www.ingramcontent.com/pod-product-compliance
Lightning Source LLC
Chambersburg PA
CBHW070058080526
44586CB00013B/1109